MW00355687

Endorsements

I am so excited to endorse this training manual by my friend Bishop Joe Ibojie. It could have so many titles, such as, "Living Supernaturally Naturally," "Walking in the Spirit," or "Your Journey with God." But I love its original title, as it speaks to this generation that unfortunately is full of books and movies about the dark side of the supernatural. But in this book there is light, the light of revelation from the Spirit of God through Bishop Ibojie.

Teaching us what the Bible has to say about the Holy Spirit and how we can walk in the Spirit in our daily lives, it is challenging and thought-provoking and helps us in our daily walk with the Lord. I love that it is a manual we can use on a one-to-one basis or in a small group setting. It helps us to challenge one another and keep one another accountable.

Now that you have this in your possession, hold on to it, prayerfully use it and learn from it. Jesus said in John 14:16 that He would give us another helper, the Holy Spirit, who would not only be with us, but would be in us forever. I encourage you to use this manual as a tool to develop your relationship with Jesus through the Holy Spirit.

God bless you in your walk with God and your commitment to His harvest.

—Joseph Ewen
Leader of the River Network of Church's NE Scotland, UK
Member of the International Oversight Team of Antioch Ministries International,
Waco, Texas, USA

Bishop Joe Ibojie at my last count has written over 12 books. Each book seeks to mobilize the body of Christ in their revelation gifts. This book again takes the supernatural and makes it natural. Bishop Joe has a fathers heart that creates a safe place for others to grow in the fullness of God. You will be blessed by this book.

—Dr. Sharon Stone
CI Europe

Books by Dr. Joe Ibojie

Bible-Based Dictionary of Prophetic Symbols for Every Christian—Best Seller

The Watchman

Dreams and Visions Volume 1—International Best Seller

Dreams and Visions Volume 2—Best Seller

The Justice of God: Victory in Everyday Living

The Final Frontiers

How to Live the Supernatural Life in the Here and Now—International Best Seller

Illustrated Bible-Based Dictionary of Dream Symbols—International Best Seller

Destined for the Top

Times of Refreshing Volume 1

Times of Refreshing Volume 2

Times of Refreshing Volume 3

Revelation Training Manual—NEW

HOW YOU CAN
LIVE AN EVERYDAY
SUPERNATURAL
LIFE

DR. JOE IBOJIE

Copyright © 2017–Dr. Joe Ibojie

All rights reserved. This book is protected under the copyright laws. This book may not be copied or reprinted for commercial gain or profit. The use of short quotations or occasional page copying for personal or group study is permitted and encouraged. Permission will be granted upon request. Unless otherwise identified, Scripture quotations are taken from THE HOLY BIBLE, NEW INTERNATIONAL VERSION®, NIV® Copyright © 1973, 1978, 1984, 2011 by Biblica, Inc.™ Used by permission. All rights reserved. Scripture quotations marked TLB are taken from The Living Bible; Tyndale House, 1997, © 1971 by Tyndale House Publishers, Inc. Used by permission. All rights reserved. Scripture quotations marked NKJV are taken from the New King James Version. Copyright © 1982 by Thomas Nelson, Inc. Used by permission. All rights reserved. Scripture quotations marked AMP are from the Amplified® Bible. Copyright © 1954, 1958, 1962, 1964, 1965, 1987 by The Lockman Foundation. Used by permission. Scripture quotations marked KJV are from the King James Version. All emphasis within Scripture quotations is the author's own. Please note that Destiny Image's publishing style capitalizes certain pronouns in Scripture that refer to the Father, Son, and Holy Spirit, and may differ from some publishers' styles. Take note that the name satan and related names are not capitalized. We choose not to acknowledge him, even to the point of violating grammatical rules.

DESTINY IMAGE® PUBLISHERS, INC.
P.O. Box 310, Shippensburg, PA 17257-0310
"Promoting Inspired Lives."

This book and all other Destiny Image and Destiny Image Fiction books are available at Christian bookstores and distributors worldwide.

For more information on foreign distributors, call 717-532-3040.

Or reach us on the Internet: www.destinyimage.com

ISBN 13: TP 978-0-7684-4312-7

ISBN 13 EBook: 978-0-7684-4313-4

For Worldwide Distribution, Printed in the U.S.A.

1 2 3 4 5 6 7 8 9 10 11 / 22 21 20 19 18 17

Contents

Introduction

How You Can Live an Everyday Supernatural Life is a comprehensive, interactive training manual based on my best-selling books: *How to Live the Supernatural Life in the Here and Now, The Justice of God, Destined for the Top, The Final Frontiers,* and *The Watchman.* This personal tool would be the perfect complement to these books as well as a stand alone manual—allowing you to glean as much wisdom as possible from what God has shared with me.

Life is simply a timed-framed experience of our spirits in this earthly abode; it is made up of moments, like turning the pages of a photo album. Our memories preserve for us the relationship and events that tell the story of each of our lives, whether happy, sad, joyful, or painful. The truth is, despite the state of play of events, our lives began in the spirit and will continue eternally in the spirit.

A supernatural life is one based solely on an intimate relationship with God the Father, God the Son, and God the Holy Spirit. The apostle Paul asked the Galatians this vital question, *"After beginning with the Spirit, are you now trying to attain your goal by human effort?"* (Gal. 3:3b). I hope the truths expressed this training manual and my books that correspond with it will stand the test of time and transcend the borders of head knowledge.

It is my hope that this manual will challenge you and stir you up to a place where the printed Word of God will lift off the pages of the Bible into every fiber of your being with renewed relevance, a place where conservatism and narrow and restricted perspectives of the eternal Word of God and supernatural living will break out into daily realities.

A preview of what is presented within the following pages includes:

- How to live supernaturally every day—in every way.

- How to safeguard your divine nature, God's gift to you.

- How to avoid curses and welcome blessings.

- How the supernatural Justice of God affects your life.

- Realizing how constructive and destructive your spoken words are.

- Welcoming angels into your everyday life.

- How to defeat the evil one at the mind game.

- How you are destined for the top!

Suitable for individual use, group study, or as Sunday school discussions, *How You Can Live an Everyday Supernatural Life* will strengthen your relationship with God, your family, and church community—perhaps even the world.

PART I

LIVING THE SUPERNATURAL LIFE

HOW YOU CAN LIVE AN EVERYDAY SUPERNATURAL LIFE

CHAPTER 1

Living the Supernatural

Above the Natural

 POINTS TO NOTE

1. Supernatural living is living above the natural and can be likened to regaining the life that Adam and Eve lost in the Garden of Eden. The natural habitat of humankind was in the Garden before the Fall, where experiential knowledge of God's presence and glory permeated the air alongside a level of intimacy allowing for a perpetual reception of divine revelation and impartation. A state of continuous God consciousness.

2. Whenever there is a repeated encounter with God, your spirit is strengthened with divine wisdom, knowledge, and revelation, and gradually imbibes the divine nature of God.

3. Before the Fall, Adam and Eve lived in an incredibly heightened spiritual awareness; and though they lived in a natural geographical location called the Garden of Eden, their spiritual senses overwhelmed and encapsulated their natural senses, making the natural senses probably dormant and virtually inactive.

 EXERCISES

A. Do you believe in there is a supernatural way of living? Is this lifestyle one that you would welcome? Why or why not?

Discussion

_____

_____

_____

B. Have you had repeated encounters with God? Occasional encounters? Rare encounters? How strong is your spirit?

Discussion

_____

_____

_____

C. Are you natural or your spiritual senses stronger? What can you do to strength your spiritual senses?

Discussion

_____

_____

_____

∽⌒∾⌒∿

Living in Two Worlds—The Reality

POINTS TO NOTE

1. We live in two worlds. The natural world is full of sin, wickedness, and all sorts of vile things that are against the knowledge of God, of which the prince of the air and the ruler of the generation is the devil and his evil system (see Rom. 1:29-31). There is also a spiritual world—the world within each believer—a place where you can see the unlimited and unrestricted insights of the beauty of His holiness and the wonders of His love and behold His infinite creativity and wisdom that abounds in His presence.

2. In reality believers struggle between the two worlds. The apostle Paul summed up this struggle in this statement, *"For I have the desire to do what is good, but I cannot carry it out. For what I do is not the good I want to do; no, the evil I do not want to do—this I keep on doing. Now if I do what I do not want to do, it is no longer I who do it, but it is sin living in me that does it* (Romans 7:18b-20).

3. God is in the process of bringing humanity back to the way it was in the Garden of Eden so we will not be bound by the intrigues and ploys of this vile and perishing world. We must submit and cooperate with the plans and purposes of God so we can regain what was lost—personally and corporately.

EXERCISES

A. Is the natural world and the spiritual world within each believer clearly defined in your mind?

Discussion

_____

_____

_____

B. If Apostle Paul struggled with the two worlds, is there any hope for believers today? Explain your answer.

Discussion

_____

_____

_____

C. How willing are you to submit and cooperate with the plans and purposes God has for your life?

Discussion

_____

_____

_____

⚬⚭⚬

Tripartite Beings

 POINTS TO NOTE

1. Humanity exists in a state of conflict of interest, which the Bible speaks of when it says, *"For the flesh lusts against the Spirit, and the Spirit against the flesh; and these are contrary to one another..."* (Gal. 5:17 NKJV). To truly become the redeemed of the Lord, we need to understand the origin of our tripartite nature and intentionally bring these warring parts under the rule of the Spirit of God (see 1 Thess. 5:23).

2. The *body* is the mortal, material part of a human being that is formed from the dust of the earth. This is the seat of the natural realm in you and is where physical interactions with the fallen world take place.

3. The *human spirit* is the immortal, nonmaterial part of a human being, formed from the breath of God. This is the seat of the spiritual realm, your center and the cardinal means of communion with God.

4. The *soul* is the mortal, nonmaterial part of a human being that provides means of interaction between the body and the spirit. This is the seat of your relational issues.

 **EXERCISES**

A. Have you ever considered the fact that you live in a constant state of conflict of interest? Have you ever intentionally brought your struggle under the rule of the Spirit of God?

Discussion

_____

_____

_____

B. Do you live mainly in the physical world, using your natural senses to guide you?

Discussion

_____

_____

_____

C. Do you allow your human spirit, formed from the breath of God, to rule your decisions, actions, speech, etc.?

Discussion

_____

_____

_____

D. How soul-conscience are you? Are you aware of the relationship between your body and your spirit?

Discussion

_____

_____

_____

Understanding Our Spirit Selves

 POINTS TO NOTE

1. Your spirit is formed from the breath of God (see Gen. 2:7; Zech. 12:1; Job 33:4).

2. King Solomon wondered where the spirit returns to at the end of a person's tenure on earth (see Eccl. 3:21). Later he confirmed that *"the dust* [body] *returns to the ground it came from, and the spirit returns to God who gave it"* (Eccl. 12:7).

3. Jesus Christ laid credence to this when He said, *"'Father, into Your hands I commit my spirit.' When He had said this, He breathed His last"* (Luke 23:46). It is therefore clear from these passages that your spirit comes from God and will return to Him for judgment when death occurs.

 EXERCISES

A. Do you feel as though you have been formed from the breath of God? Why or why not?

Discussion

_____

_____

_____

B. Do you believe that your body will cease to exist but that your spirit will exist forever with God?

Discussion

_____

_____

_____

C. What do you think about Judgment Day? Are you looking forward to it—or dreading it?

Discussion

_____

_____

_____

༄༅

The Trilogy of the Spirit

 POINTS TO NOTE

1. The most important part of us is our spirit. Our spirit comes from God and will return to Him. It's the part of us created in the likeness and image of God. The three functional components of the spirit are: 1) divine wisdom, 2) sanctified conscience, and 3) communion with God. When our flesh is crucified, the spirit can come to its fullness in God.

2. The spirit is our center and operates through revelations (the soul operates through information). We commune with God mainly through the spirit. *"God is Spirit, and those who worship Him must worship in spirit and truth"* (John 4:24 NKJV). Our spirits bear witness with the Spirit of God. The strength of the human spirit is its capacity to bear witness with the Spirit of God from whom it came.

3. From the fallen state to our redemption, the human spirit exists at two levels: *unregenerate spirit*—our spirit in the fallen state. And *regenerated spirit*—the born-again Christian's state; our spirit after redemption by the blood of Jesus Christ.

 EXERCISES

A. Of the three components of the spirit, which do you mostly readily identify with? Which is the strongest within you? How crucified is your flesh?

Discussion

_____

_____

_____

B. What is the difference between communing with God in your spirit and connecting with God in another way?

Discussion

_____

_____

_____

C. How strong is your regenerated spirit? Does it rule your mind? Or vice versa?

Discussion

_____

_____

_____

Spiritual Senses

 POINTS TO NOTE

1. Spiritual senses are the senses that are operative from our spirit, also known as the senses of our faith. The natural senses are senses operative from our natural body and are limited in the dimensions of time, space, height, and depth. However, there are no limitations with perception using the pure and unpolluted spiritual senses.

2. Words of knowledge (which reveal from the past and the present and prophecy which speaks of the future) are discerned with spiritual senses. Prophetic utterances are also multidimensional in dynamics and are perceived using spiritual senses.

3. In the coming days, many people will receive healing and deliverance in their dreams and visions, and many others will be significantly imparted to in the arena of divine spiritual encounters. Spiritual senses transcend the limits of the human mind and natural senses.

 EXERCISES

A. How sensitive are your senses of faith (your spiritual senses)? What can you do to hone them?

Discussion

_____

_____

_____

B. Do you receive dreams and visions? Have you received a word of knowledge? How open is your spirit to these types of communication from God?

Discussion

_____

_____

_____

C. How probable do you think it is to "receive healing and deliverance" during a dream?

Discussion

_____

_____

_____

⧁∾⧂

Strengthening Your Spirit and Spiritual Senses

POINTS TO NOTE

1. The way to cooperate with God is to learn to live in the spirit. To live in the spirit or supernatural, we must first train ourselves for spiritual fitness. We have learned to develop the soul and the body, mostly at the expense of the spirit. Teaching about the need to exercise our spirit is rare, even though the Bible clearly admonishes us to do so in First Timothy 4:7-8 (TLB).

2. Our *natural conscience* recognizes between right and wrong regarding conduct, together with the feeling that we ought not to do wrong. But when we allow God to teach us the true way of life, we strengthen our human spirit. A sanctified natural conscience is the one washed by the blood of Jesus.

3. Our *sanctified conscience* is therefore superior to our natural conscience. When we apply our sanctified conscience, by being less self-conscious and more God-centered, we strengthen our spirit. Another way to empower our spirit is to use the wisdom of God, which is the "life's application of the Word of God." The only true wisdom is following the dictates of the commandments of God, no matter what.

EXERCISES

A. On a scale of one to ten, how spiritually fit are you? Are you a champion athlete, totally out of shape, or somewhere between?

Discussion

_____

_____

_____

B. Is your natural conscience on duty at all times or does it take a break when you are facing hard decisions?

Discussion

_____

_____

_____

C. Having a sanctified conscience brings a God-centered attitude and mindset rather than a selfish self-consciousness. How sanctified is your conscience?

Discussion

_____

_____

_____

ာာာ

Operating Less from the Soul Realm

POINTS TO NOTE

1. In the routines of life, your spirit becomes strong if you operate less from the soul realm. Whenever you spend time with God, you become less emotional; the more you apply the Word of God (which is divine wisdom), the less you depend on human will.

2. The more you use your sanctified conscience—laying aside personal agenda and learning to prefer others—the less dependent you become on the human mind and the rule of head-knowledge.

EXERCISES

A. Many people are labeled "emotional." Have you been accused of this? How apt are you at applying the Word of God to your everyday situations?

Discussion

_____

_____

_____

B. For some people, thinking of others seems to be very natural for them. How natural—or supernatural—is it for you to lay aside your personal agenda and concentrate more on others?

Discussion

_____

_____

_____

⋘⋙

Sharp and Sensitive Spiritual Senses

POINTS TO NOTE

1. In practical terms, to be strong in the spirit means to overcome temptations, make wise and timely decisions, receive God's ideas and reject evil ideas, witness the Good News, and ultimately, to allow God to use you as a vessel of honor.

2. When the spirit is strong, the spiritual senses become sharp and sensitive. Actually, you are only as strong as your spirit. The spirit must be reborn, the mind must be renewed, and the body must be brought under control. Paul said, "I die every day"; meaning the flesh continuously tries to resurrect (see also Eph. 3:16-17).

3. The Bible uses the word *spirit* in two ways: 1) *Spirit* as a supernatural being, whether divine, human, or evil. 2) *Spirit* as one's mood or disposition, or an attitude (figurative use of the word *spirit*); see Proverbs 15:13, 16:32, 18:1. In this manual the use of word spirit refers to the former.

EXERCISES

A. Do you overcome temptations most of the time? Some of the time? Rarely? How about making wise and timely decisions? Receiving God's ideas and rejecting evil ideas? Witnessing the Good News? Allowing God to use you as His vessel of honor?

Discussion

_____

_____

_____

B. Are your spiritual senses sharp and sensitive—or dull?

Discussion

_____

_____

_____

C. What does the word spirit mean to you? How does the human spirit differ from the Holy Spirit?

Discussion

_____

_____

_____

೧৴৹

PRACTICAL PRINCIPLES AND DISCUSSION

_____

_____

_____

_____

_____

_____

_____

_____

_____

_____

_____

CHAPTER 2

Living in the Spirit

The Sanctified Mind

 POINTS TO NOTE

The cardinal pivots for living in the spirit are; a sanctified mind, a personal will yielded to God, a born-again spirit and inner peace.

1. A sanctified mind is a prerequisite for living a successful supernatural life. We must understand the dynamics of our thought processes to correctly channel them for the purposes of God. Our thoughts determine the outcome of our lives. We need to choose and constantly reflect on what we think.

2. A passive mind is a dangerous mind because it submits to every external agent without resistance. It will go with the flow of the body, but the flow of the body is fickle and unduly influences choices. Remember, life is about the choices you make.

3. You need to have a positive mindset. The Bible speaks of this: *"For who has known the mind of the Lord that he may instruct Him? But we have the mind of Christ"* (1 Cor. 2:16). Do not give any chances to the enemy to darken your mind (see Rom. 1:21). Set your mind on things above (see Col. 3:2-3) by setting your mind on the right things. Your mind should be under the rule of the Spirit of God.

 EXERCISES

A. Do you seriously consider the things you think about, ponder? Do you constantly choose to reflect on what is going through your mind?

Discussion

_____

_____

_____

B. What do you consider to be a "passive mind"? What it he difference between a passive mind, an assertive mind, and an aggressive mind? How would you define your mind?

Discussion

_____

_____

_____

C. How can you tell when the enemy has darkened your mind? What ways have you used to keep the enemy out and let righteousness in?

Discussion

_____

_____

_____

⤸⤷

A Yielded Personal Will

 POINTS TO NOTE

1. Living in the Spirit and living a life in the flesh are the opposite poles of God's measurement. One is diametrically opposed to the other. The basis for a supernatural spiritual life is captured by Apostle Paul's statement, *"I say then: Walk in the Spirit, and you shall not fulfill the lust of the flesh"* (Gal. 5:16 NKJV).

2. At one end of the spectrum is the lust of the flesh (see Eph. 2:3-5 NKJV), and on the other end is the life we now live as Christians (see Col. 2:6-9). Somehow between these two ends is a point in time when we became translated into His wonderful and marvelous Kingdom. This transformation began at the point of salvation, and is continued throughout life.

3. If you deny, refuse, or rebuff the desires of the flesh willfully and for long enough, they become weaker and weaker and eventually almost imperceptible; they will no longer rule your life. The eventual rule of the Spirit of God in your life comes down to the struggle between *the will of God* and *your will* in the daily routines of life. By giving up the desires of the flesh, you gain a Spirit-led life.

 **EXERCISES**

A. Think of two examples when you walked in the flesh rather than the spirit. Now think of two examples when you walked in the spirit rather than the flesh. What were the outcomes of those four situations?

Discussion

_____

_____

_____

B. *Therefore, my dear friends...continue to work out your salvation with fear and trembling, for it is God who works in you to will and to act according to His good purpose* (Philippians 2:12-13). Are you continuing to work out your salvation?

Discussion

_____

_____

_____

C. In the daily struggle between the will of God and your will, which will claims the most victories?

Discussion

_____

_____

_____

∽∾∾

The Reborn Spirit

 POINTS TO NOTE

1. The struggle of wills is similar to what Jesus went through in the Garden of Gethsemane: *"My Father, if it is possible, may this cup be taken from Me. Yet not as I will, but as You will"* (Matt. 26:39). Once the will of God is allowed to stand, as Jesus did in His humanity, the power of the flesh is diminished, and life in the Spirit becomes easier and more enjoyable.

2. When your spirit is reborn, the plug is pulled from the grip of the flesh and its yearnings. From this point on, the born-again Christian is able to strengthen his or her spirit, making the spirit more sensitive to the prompting of the Spirit of God. When we are born again, the Spirit of the Lord Himself enters our lives and brings liberty and abundance with the transforming power of Christ within us.

3. As a result of being born-again, circumstances that would have stripped us of hope, joy, and courage instead become opportunities to exercise faith, employ love, and trust God. We are empowered to see things through the supernatural eyes of faith, transcending the limits of natural understanding.

 EXERCISES

A. After reading Matthew 26:39, does it seem to you that Jesus was having second thoughts about going through with His humiliation, torture, crucifixion, and death?

Discussion

_____

_____

_____

B. Are you 100 percent positive that you are a born-again Christian? Why or why not?

Discussion

_____

_____

_____

C. Can you supernaturally see hope, joy, and courage while going through challenges and troubles? Do you see each trial as an opportunity to exercise your faith, employ love, and trust God?

Discussion

_____

_____

_____

ভেদ্ম

Inner Peace

 POINTS TO NOTE

1. Keeping your peace is a priority for living in the spirit. Real peace is a gift from God, a product of your relationship with Him. It is the will of God that you have peace (see Col. 1:19-20). Without peace, your experience in God will be limited. Peace will enable you to know who you are in Christ and who Christ is to you, and also who the Holy Spirit is to you, especially on your worst, most disagreeable days.

2. World events of recent times are a reflection of the battle in the heavenlies, the unseen realm. If our peace is predicated on human reasoning, it most likely does not come from the Holy Spirit, for the peace of God surpasses all understanding (see Rom. 14:17-19).

3. Two essential elements of the Kingdom of God, peace and joy, elude most Christians. Peace is a priority and joy is a prerequisite for supernatural living by the Spirit. The first thing the enemy wants to steal is your peace, followed by your joy. If he succeeds, then he plants doubts in your subconscious mind.

 EXERCISES

A. How peaceful are you? Your thoughts? Your dreams? Your expectations for the future?

Discussion

_____

_____

_____

B. Can you say with certainty that deep down you have a peace that passes all understanding?

Discussion

_____

_____

_____

C. Has the enemy incessantly intruded into your mind to the point where you were unable to focus on God and His love for you? What did you do to counteract his tactics?

Discussion

_____

_____

_____

Supernatural Peace

 POINTS TO NOTE

1. Peace is a powerful weapon of spiritual warfare; the enemy is after it, and you need to hold on to it. The best way to fight the enemy is not on the ground he has chosen, but on the dictates from God; when you engage the enemy too quickly, you end up fighting for the wrong reason.

2. Without peace, recourse to resentment, bitterness, and revenge, rather than intercessory spiritual warfare, is more likely. You cannot rely on your feelings to determine the measure of the peace you enjoy. Feelings are fickle and you need to rely on your spirit.

3. If the enemy steals your peace, he will cloud your soul and your ability to make wise and godly decisions. Life is decision driven. Whatever affects your decision making will control your experiences in life and ultimately impinge on the fulfilment of your destiny

 EXERCISES

A. Have you ever thought of using peace as a spiritual weapon? If not, how do you think it will affect the enemy? Is the enemy confused when you hold your peace instead of being agitated?

Discussion

_____

_____

_____

B. If you have no peace within, how do you react without? How fickle are your feelings? Are you riding an emotional rollercoaster most days?

Discussion

_____

_____

_____

C. How does lack of peace affect your decision making processes? If you are in turmoil, rather than peaceful, are your decisions going to be tainted, off balance?

Discussion

_____

_____

_____

⤜⤛

Hold Your Peace

POINTS TO NOTE

1. For God to fight for you, you must hold your peace. Stillness is necessary for God to act on your behalf (see Ps. 46:10). Stillness does not mean not doing anything; it means calmness in your inner being while your outer being is working things out.

2. Anything that comes against the capacity to hold peace is the *spirit of strife*, a weapon that the enemy uses quite often. The enemy sends this evil spirit to delude, destabilize, and demoralize; then it gradually penetrates your defenses. If the spirit of strife is discerned, resist it and make all efforts to be at peace no matter what.

3. Spend quiet time with God in the midst of the opposition to get further clarity and a fresh mandate. This stage of the battle is crucial and is known as silent warfare. When you hold your peace, God is at work and the enemy is confused and defeated.

EXERCISES

A. Is it easy or difficult for you to remain calm inside when outside circumstances are chaotic?

Discussion

_____

_____

_____

B. Have you ever felt an evil spirit trying to delude, destabilize, and demoralize you? Did it gradually penetrate your defenses? How did you overcome it?

Discussion

_____

_____

_____

C. How often do you spend quiet time with God? Should you increase that time by 10, 50, 100 percent?

Discussion

_____

_____

_____

∽∽∽

Practicing Peace

 POINTS TO NOTE

1. The degree to which you worry is the degree to which you do not know God. This was why the first thing God said to Gideon after he was visited by the angel was, *"Peace! Do not be afraid. You are not going to die.' So Gideon built an altar to the Lord there and called it The Lord is Peace"* (Judges 6:23-24a). Peace is a reflection of our trust and confidence in God.

2. Troubles will come; but what matters is your ability to confront issues and still retain your peace. The measure of your supernatural living is determined by how quickly it takes you to regain your balance on the day that evil attacks. For some it takes minutes, hours, or days; for others it might take weeks, months, or even forever. The key to practicing peace is to persevere until you master the quickest way to return to peace on an evil day.

3. You must see things from the measure of grace God has made available to you, not from the evil that comes your way. Fear and panic are products of human logic, so you must intentionally avoid the work of the soul—the emotion, the will, and the mind—and retreat into your spirit.

 **EXERCISES**

A. Are you a worrier? Perhaps you come from a long line of worriers in your family? What does worrying indicate about your relationship with Jesus, your Savior.

Discussion

_____

_____

_____

B. When troubles come your way, do they knock you off your feet and keep you down for days? Weeks? Years? Are there some troubles you may take along to your grave if you don't take action now to solve them?

Discussion

_____

_____

_____

C. Fear and panic are products of human logic. How often do you give in to this tactic of the enemy? To avoid the work of the soul—the emotion, the will, and the mind—do you often retreat into your spirit?

Discussion

_____

_____

_____

PRACTICAL PRINCIPLES AND DISCUSSION

CHAPTER 3

Divine Safeguards for a Supernatural Life

Testing the Spirits

 POINTS TO NOTE

1. Most people, as they desire live a supernatural life in the spirit, wonder how to recognize the counterfeit power of the devil. This is a legitimate question and should be the concern of everyone learning to walk in the spirit. There are many voices in the spirit world. Many gifted people are today in the service of the enemy because they have unknowingly allowed their gifts and abilities to be hijacked by the satanic system.

2. Though satan can neither tell the future nor give revelation, he is a master in information shifting and he masquerades as the angel of light. The following is a useful safeguard in your personal walk in the spirit. Always remember this quick test: Does it draw you closer to God? Does it exalt Jesus Christ? Does it respect all human life? And does it speak of love?

3. When speaking of the signs of the times and the end of the age, Jesus Christ said, *"Watch out that no one deceives you. For many will come in My name, claiming, 'I am the Christ,' and will deceive many"* (Matt. 24:4-5). He later said, *"For false Christs and false prophets will appear and perform great signs and miracles to deceive even the elect—if that were possible"* (Matt. 24:24).

 EXERCISES

A. Have you ever wondered how to recognize the counterfeit power of the devil?

Discussion

_____

_____

_____

B. Do you think these are good questions to ask yourself to safeguard your personal spiritual walk: Does it draw you closer to God? Does it exalt Jesus Christ? Does it respect all human life? And does it speak of love?

Discussion

_____

_____

_____

C. Do you take Jesus' warnings seriously? Have you personally witnessed or heard of deceivers, false christs, and false prophets?

Discussion

_____

_____

_____

Test Questions

 POINTS TO NOTE

1. John admonishes us to ascertain the source of the spirit that is manifesting in any given circumstance, _"Do not believe every spirit, but test the spirits to see whether they are from God"_ (1 John 4:1). Does it acknowledge Jesus? if it doesn't then it is from the spirit of this world (devil). To test a spirit means to examine the gifts (what the spirit does) and evaluate the fruit (the nature, attributes, or what the spirit stands for) of the spirit, before believing it. Every genuine spiritual experience should endorse the reality of God's love as revealed in Scripture.

2. Testing the human spirit starts with you. Examine yourself and see what kind of spirit you are operating in. The Bible says, _"Examine yourselves to see whether you are in the faith; test yourselves. Do you not realize that Christ Jesus is in you—unless, of course, you fail the test?"_ (2 Cor. 13:5). Check your motivation, your drive and your goals. This test of faith is to ensure that Jesus Christ dwells in you. You should then test the spirit behind your actions and decisions.

3. Put the action or decision through the "time-test"; anything that cannot wait is not of God, for God is patient. Is it self-promoting? Does it especially appeal to the ego? If it does, then it is most probably not of God. Does it lead to mutual peace? No matter how smart an idea is, if it does not lead to peace, it is not from God, for God is peace.

 **EXERCISES**

D. Do you always examine the gifts (what the spirit does) and evaluate the fruit (the nature, attributes, or what the spirit stands for) of the spirit, before believing what someone tells you or something you "feel" the Lord told you?

Discussion

_____

_____

_____

E. Do you routinely examine yourself to see what kind of spirit you are operating in? Do you regularly test the spirit behind your actions and decisions?

Discussion

_____

_____

_____

F. Does knowing that God is patient, not self-promoting, and brings mutual peace help you determine if the spirit is from God or from the enemy?

Discussion

_____

_____

_____

⚜

More Testing

 POINTS TO NOTE

1. Test the spirits of other people along the same lines as testing the spirit behind your own actions and decisions. Irrespective of the strength of your spirit, the spirits of other people do impact on you in one way or the other.

2. There should be guided interaction between your spirit and the spirits of other people, even when both are borne of God, because first you hear or see in part; and second, there is no substitute to receiving directly from God.

3. If an action or decision is compulsive, or if it drives the person, then it is of this world. Also, if it pushes a person, controls the person, or leaves the person with self-condemnation, lack of peace, hostility, bitterness, envy, or unforgiveness, then it is of the world. Finally, does it draw the person away from God? If it does, then it is also borne of the spirit of the world, which is the enemy (see Gal. 5:19-21).

 EXERCISES

A. Are you easily influenced by other people? Your parents? Your spouse? Your children? Co-workers? Church friends?

    Discussion

    _____

    _____

    _____

B. Are you sometimes guilty of relying more on friends and family rather than God?

    Discussion

    _____

    _____

    _____

C. *"The acts of the sinful nature are obvious: sexual immorality, impurity and debauchery; idolatry and witch-craft; hatred, discord, jealousy, fits of rage, selfish ambition, dissensions, factions and envy; drunkenness, orgies, and the like. I warn you, as I did before, that those who live like this will not inherit the kingdom of God"* (Gal. 5:19-21). Apostle Paul was frankly honest in this Scripture passage. Are you as honest in your interpretation of it?

    Discussion

    _____

    _____

    _____

Additional Safeguards

 POINTS TO NOTE

1. Be rooted in the Word of God to determine the source of the spirit (see Col. 1:24-29).

2. You must live in the love of God (see Col. 2:1-3; Isa. 60:2; Eph. 3:17-19; 1 John 4:8).

3. Remain firm in your faith (see Col. 2:4-5; Jer. 1:5).

4. Live in Him (see Col. 2:6-7; Neh. 6:1-4; Heb. 12:1-2; Acts 17:28).

5. Avoid the principles of the world (see Col. 2:8).

6. Remain connected to Christ; grow in God and in fellowship with other saints (see Col. 2:9-10,19).

7. Live in the righteousness of God (see Col. 2:13-15).

8. Avoid the religious system (see Col. 2:16-17).

9. Avoid the spirit of false humility and undue dependence on human command and sensual indulgence (see Col. 2:18, 20-23; Rom. 2:28-29).

 EXERCISES

A. Of the nine additional safeguards, which ones are you most willing to abide by? Which are the hardest to implement?

Discussion

_____

_____

_____

B. Do you find comfort or condemnation in "fellowshipping with other saints"?

Discussion

_____

_____

_____

C. What does it mean to you to "live in Him"?

Discussion

_____

_____

_____

∽∾∽

Practical Principles and Discussion

∽ **PRACTICAL PRINCIPLES AND DISCUSSION** ∽

_____

_____

_____

_____

_____

_____

_____

_____

_____

_____

_____

_____

_____

_____

_____

CHAPTER 4

Danger Zones

Spiritual Drifting From God

 POINTS TO NOTE

1. The main danger of spiritual drifting is how it subtly creeps into the lives of its victims. Drifting is the quiet, gradual, slow, blind, and unintentional slipping away from the values of Christianity, and it is the result of a multitude of small and seemingly insignificant excuses. People do not drift upward, they drift downward! Moving toward God is done on purpose and is a deliberate and conscious effort.

2. The evil of spiritual drifting is menacing and basks on the bed of compromise and procrastination. God's grace is truly beyond measure, but we must not receive this grace in vain. Therefore, continuously come to Him, just as Job did when he offered sacrifice on behalf of his children (see Job 1:5). People drift because they neglect spending quality time with God, through prayerlessness, lack of focus, and influence by the affairs of the world.

3. Another danger of spiritual drifting involves a passion or giftedness that is not properly harnessed, which eventually leads to perversion. Solomon eventually became perverted (also see Mal. 2:1-2). Everyone will drift from God at some point in time, but we must make the decision to reverse the trend.

 EXERCISES

A. Have you drifted away from God?

Discussion

_____

_____

_____

B. Are you lying in a bed of compromise and procrastination?

Discussion

_____

_____

_____

C. Do you know anyone with perverted passion or gift? Or has your passion or giftedness been perverted?

Discussion

_____

_____

_____

❧❧❧

Sexual Sins Subvert Spirituality

POINTS TO NOTE

1. Sexual desire is easily the most common idol in the hearts of men and women. Time and time again, God allegorized the sin of idolatry with the sin of sexual promiscuity and immorality. The prophet Jeremiah graphically compared the sin of idolatry to sexual promiscuity (see Jer. 2:20 and Hosea 1:2). See also Jeremiah 3:6.

2. Sexual bondage is peculiar. It creeps in subtly, but grips with so much intensity, overwhelming its victims with such a passion, that reason and logic are easily thrown into the abyss. This addiction can be traced to humanity's image center, the pictorial depository of our imagination. The grip and enticement of pictures in our imagination is hard to suppress and the addiction difficult to overcome.

3. *Sanctified imagination* is important for receiving and handling revelations from God whereas corrupted imagination, emanating from sexual sin, pollutes the imagination which blurs and distorts the seer's reception. Do not allow sexual sin or inordinate sexual indulgence to subvert your walk with God. When Israel posed a military threat to Moab, the Moabites, on the advice of Balam, used this age-long vulnerability to sexual sin to subvert Israel's spirituality.

EXERCISES

A. Have you fallen prey to sexual perversion?

Discussion

_____

_____

_____

B. What visions are in your imagination? Righteous visions or perverted images?

Discussion

_____

_____

_____

C. What steps can you take to keep a sanctified imagination?

Discussion

_____

_____

_____

⚜

Spiritual Cockiness

 POINTS TO NOTE

1. It is spiritual cockiness to think that our little part is the whole story. This evil has led to the fall of many anointed people in the Kingdom of God, and it can come in various forms and shapes.

2. Spiritual cockiness also involves other attitudes and subsequent actions, such as looking down on what God is doing through other people, or using the power of your spirituality without restraint, or giving your personal opinion as if it is God's opinion.

3. It is also spiritual cockiness to neglect revelatory guidance from God because we do not personally receive the revelation. To disregard our spouse's or children's revelations because we think we are "more spiritually mature," is spiritual cockiness—and this is dangerous.

EXERCISES

A. When reading these points, did someone you know come to mind? Or did you personally consider these points regarding your own life?

Discussion

_____

_____

_____

B. Have you ever thought about or actually given your opinion as if it was God's opinion?

Discussion

_____

_____

_____

C. Do you know people who act as if they are more spiritually mature that you are? How do you react to these people?

Discussion

_____

_____

_____

CHAPTER 5

God Speaks in Many Ways

 POINTS TO NOTE

1. God speaks to us in a variety of ways: through the Bible; through dreams, visions, trances, visitations, and translations; through audible voice; and through other people.

2. Here are four ways people hear the voice of God. Some are *hearers*—their gift is predominantly in the ability to hear what God is saying. Some are *feelers*—they feel what God wants to communicate, for example, as pains in the part of the body where God wants to heal somebody. Some are *seers*—they are gifted in the ability to see pictures, flashes of pictures, and dreams and visions on a constant basis. Others are *spiritually sensitive* enough to discern what God is saying by the spirit of discernment.

3. There are many voices in the spirit world, but the voice of God is recognizable only if the message is subjected to the following checks. Does the message:

    - Lead you to greater intimacy with God?

    - Lead to expression of love? (For God is love.)

    - Put God's benefit and the interest of others before personal benefit?

    - Lead to greater manifestations of Christ-likeness?

    - Lead to more humility? Or does it appeal to the ego?

    - Generate more joy, peace, and righteousness? (The Kingdom of God is love, peace, and righteousness in the Holy Spirit.)

    - Lead to greater dependence on God?

    - Line up with the written Word of God? If it does, it's likely a message from God.

EXERCISES

A. How many different ways has God spoken to you?

Discussion

_____

_____

_____

B. How would you define yourself? As a hearer, feeler, seer, or spiritually sensitive? Why?

Discussion

_____

_____

_____

C. Can you think of additional checks you could use to ensure the message is from God/

Discussion

_____

_____

_____

Revelation Versus Information

 POINTS TO NOTE

1. All revelations come from God, for revelation is divine insight. Revelation is the flash of illumination from Heaven on the established truths of God (see Hab. 2:3).

2. The enemy does not give revelation, as he is radically opposed to the illumination of the truths of God. Instead, his preoccupation is to twist or darken the established truths of God.

3. Information, on the other hand, is the product of human wisdom and is knowledge-based. The enemy is a master at shifting information through a vast network, and he often masquerades information as revelation.

4. To treat information as revelation is futile, for information is fallible and revelation is not. revelation does not lie, though our understanding may sometimes be wrong. It is the sovereign choice of God, whether to give revelation or not. God determines when to give revelation, who to give revelation to, and what to reveal. Revelation transcends the limits of time and is more powerful than information.

 EXERCISES

A. If all revelations come from God, how important is it for you to be focused on Him at all times?

Discussion

_____

_____

_____

B. Why do you think it is the enemy's goal to keep your focus off God and on yourself?

Discussion

_____

_____

_____

C. Have you ever mistaken information for revelation? When and why?

Discussion

_____

_____

_____

❦

Why Revelations?

 POINTS TO NOTE

1. There is power inherent in revelations; the keys of the authority of the Kingdom of God.

2. Revelations come from the Father in heaven, the throne of God (see Matt. 16:13-20). Revelation does not come from human ideology, history, traditions or imagination.

3.   Revelations come with inherent potentials and power to:

- Bless

- Illuminate the established truths of God

- Be the foundation on which God establishes His Church

- Be the solid rock of standard for Christianity

- Give the keys or authority of heaven

- Defeat the enemy and the gates of hell cannot prevail against it

- Link the heaven and the earth

- Bind on earth and whatever it binds on earth will be bound in heaven

- Loose on earth, and whatever is loosed on earth will be loosed in heaven

 EXERCISES

A.   Why are revelations from God important when living a supernatural lifestyle?

Discussion

_____

_____

_____

B.   Have you been a recipient of the listed potentials and powers? Do you realize this can be your everyday way of living?

Discussion

_____

_____

_____

God Speaks Through Nature, Events, Circumstances

 POINTS TO NOTE

1. The voice of nature and the mundane routines of life can be heard clearly. Valuable lessons are available from nature and the ordinary events and circumstances that confront us. God often speaks through nature, events, and circumstances (see Ps. 19:1-4).

2. One of the most common and also most easily missed ways God speaks to us is through events that are acted out in front of us. Nothing happens by accident (see 2 Tim. 2:15). Most events and circumstances are so divinely orchestrated, not only to speak to us, but also to leave a lasting melody in our consciousness long after the events have ended (see Prov. 24:30-32).

 EXERCISES

A. How attuned are you to nature and your surroundings? Can you slow your pace enough to enjoy the natural beauty of the ordinary—lush green grass, a gentle breeze, a baby blue sky.

Discussion

_____

_____

_____

B. Nothing happens by accident. Do you really believe this? Why or why not?

Discussion

_____

_____

_____

C. Exercise 3 quote proverbs 24:30-32

God Speaks Through Signs, Miracles, Wonders

 POINTS TO NOTE

1. Just as God speaks through nature, He may also interrupt the natural to bring something to your notice. *Signs* are signals from God that point to the presence or existence of a fact or condition that is not immediately evident from the natural (see Acts 2:19).

2. A *miracle* is an event that appears unexplained by the laws of nature and so is held to be supernatural in origin or an act of God. A *wonder* is defined as that which arouses awe, astonishment or admiration, or something strange.

3. Whether a divine sign, a wonder, or a miracle, they all transcend the limits of natural logic; and they confirm the supernaturalness, supremacy, and sovereignty of God (see Dan. 4:3 and Exod. 4:8). Though divine signs are supernatural signals from Heaven, they happen in the natural and are therefore easily missed.

 EXERCISES

A. Have you received a sign from God? What was it? How did you feel? What was your reaction?

Discussion

_____

_____

_____

B. Have you received a miracle or a wonder from God? What were they? How did you feel? What was your reaction? Quote Exodus 4:8 - 'the voice of sign

Discussion

_____

_____

_____

C. Do you think you have missed some signs, miracles, and wonders that God sent to you because you were distracted by worldly endeavors?

Discussion

_____

_____

_____

The Value of Signs, Wonders, and Miracles

 POINTS TO NOTE

1. Divine signs, miracles, and wonders reveal the glory of God (see John 2:11). They draw attention to something we otherwise would have missed. They increase our faith in God and draw us closer to Him (see John 2:22). They establish the authority and sovereignty of God (see John 2:18).

2. It is important to remember, however, *that signs are not the seal of divinity. For false Christs and false prophets will appear and perform great signs and miracles to deceive even the elect—if that were possible"* (Matthew 24:24).

3. Angels are continuously involved in the planning, arranging, and executing of your circumstances so you can maximize your benefits arising from the signs from God. When you respond to divine signs, God rewards every action you take.

 EXERCISES

A. Do you welcome signs, miracles, and wonders into your life—or are you apprehensive or afraid?

Discussion

_____

_____

_____

B. What does Matthew 24:24 mean to you? Write the verse in your own words.

Discussion

_____

_____

_____

C. Do you believe that angels are gifts from God to help you in your daily living?

Discussion

_____

_____

_____

God Speaks Through The Logo Word

 POINTS TO NOTE

1. God will speak to us in many others ways, but one of the main ways is through the written Word of God (see 2 Tim. 3:16-17). Not everyone goes in the same direction at a crossroad; each person needs to understand what God is saying on a personal level to avoid a crowd mentality. This is a prerequisite for running the race that is set before you (see Heb. 1:1-2a).

2. Jesus Christ is the Word of God.

3. God may speak on a general level (what He is saying to everyone) the *logo* word; on a personal level (what He is saying to you), He speaks the *rhema* word.

4. In Romans 10:8 Paul said, *"But what does it say? 'The word is near you; it is in your mouth and in your heart,' that is, the word of faith we are proclaiming."* In real-life terms, this statement translates as the following:

    *   "Is near you" means that Christ has come from Heaven and has brought the Word to us on earth (bringing understanding and simplicity).

    *   "In your mouth" means that by the confession of the mouth the Word of God is brought to life (confession).

    *   "In your heart" means the Word is birthed by the Spirit in your heart—the *rhema* word (belief).

 EXERCISES

A. *"In the past God spoke to our forefathers through the prophets at many times and in various ways, but in these last days He has spoken to us by His Son"* (Heb. 1:1-2a). Have you heard God speaking through His Son, Jesus?

    Discussion

    _____

    _____

    _____

B. Has God spoken to you personally through a *rehma* word?

    Discussion

    _____

    _____

    _____

C. Write what Romans 10:8 means to you...personally, today, right now. Do you think your meaning will change along with the circumstances you face?

Discussion

_____

_____

_____

God Speaks Through Rhema Word

 POINTS TO NOTE

1. The *rhema* word is a word in season (see Isa. 50:4a NKJV). A *rhema* is an inspired word that is birthed within your own spirit—a whisper from the Holy Spirit like the still small voice that spoke to Elijah in the cave.

2. The strategy for your breakthrough lies in discerning the *rhema* word for your situation. Peter's obedience to what the Lord said to him on a personal level not only led him to the miraculous catch of fishes, but it was also the place where he realized what God meant to him on a day that was otherwise disagreeable. A single *rhema* word from God can change your life.

3. A *rhema* word can come to you in a variety of ways:

   - A divinely inspired word in your spirit.
   - A still small voice.
   - A divinely inspired impression upon your soul.
   - A flash of thoughts.
   - A flash of creative ideas from God.
   - A quickening *rhema* that says, "This applies to you" or "This is that."

EXERCISES

A. Has the Holy Spirit ever birthed a word from within you that illuminated your natural understanding?

Discussion

_____

_____

_____

B. Are you ready to receive a *rehma* word from God?

Discussion

_____

_____

_____

C. Considering the variety of ways listed, which way or ways does God usually speak to you?

Discussion

_____

_____

_____

❧❦❧

❧ PRACTICAL PRINCIPLES AND DISCUSSION ❧

_____

_____

_____

_____

_____

_____

CHAPTER 6

Curses

Confronting Curses with the Power of Blessings

 POINTS TO NOTE

1. One of the most common ways that evil spirits gain entrance into a person is through curses. A curse is a pronouncement or a spoken word that has some particular form of spiritual power and authority to bring limitation on a target. A curse is empowered by evil spirit, which implements the objective of the curse.

2. Blessings occur in a similar way, but the contents and purpose are very different. A blessing is the power from God to obtain the desired result in life. You can therefore break the power of curses by releasing the power of blessing as light dispels the evil of darkness.

3. Curses can be broken, but divine blessing cannot be annulled (see Isa. 10:27 NKJV). Divine blessing cannot be annulled because it is a gift from God and is therefore irrevocable (see Gen. 27:27-34). Breaking a curse supersedes deliverance because in addition to breaking the freedom of the operation of the evil spirit, it ensures that no further entrance remains for the evil spirit to use.

 EXERCISES

A. How familiar are you with curses? Do you consider curses just part of some cultures and not really applicable to you?

Discussion

_____

_____

_____

B. How blessed are you? Have you been blessed with power from God to achieve your heart's desires?

Discussion

_____

_____

_____

C. Have you had to ask God to break a curse that was holding you back from living a supernatural life?

Discussion

_____

_____

_____

⤜⤛

The Concept of Cursing

POINTS TO NOTE

1. A curse starts and exists in the *spirit* and effects its limitations by manifesting in the realm of the *physical*, possessing operational duality. For a curse to be completely broken it has to be dealt with in its twofold existence.

2. The concept of curses was introduced by God Himself in Genesis 3:17. God gave clear perimeter for the outworking of a curse: It is a consequence of a sinful action. It is specific in its targeting. It is programmed to exert a limitation on the target. It causes hardship, pain, or disfavor to the person, object, or people group—in this case it is Adam. *Sin is the origin of a curse.* When there is no sin, there will be no curse.

3. God expounded on the concept of curses (see Deut. 30:19-20), which focused on the following principles: *"Set before you life and death, blessings and curses"; "Now choose life"; "That you and your children may live";* and *"That you may love the Lord your God, listen to His voice, and hold fast to Him."*

EXERCISES

A. Can you think of a biblical example of a curse that started in the spirit then manifested in the physical realm? How about a current-day example?

Discussion

_____

_____

_____

B. Do you have to be "sin free" to be "curse free"?

Discussion

_____

_____

_____

C. When faced with life and death situations, do you choose life? Spiritual life versus worldly death? (See Revelation 22:3.)

Discussion

_____

_____

_____

⌘

Specific Outworking of Curses

 POINTS TO NOTE

1. In Deuteronomy 28:15-19, God gave further specific outworkings of how curses operate. The passage tells us how to avoid the evil of curses, that certain curses have geographical specifications, some are targeted to certain areas of life, some are gender specific, and some curses are time, event, or situation sensitive.

2. Though curses are powered by evil spirits, the parameters and mechanism of action are clearly laid down by God. Evil spirits police and implement the objectives of a curse on a person. The way evil affects limitations are revealed in the Book of Deuteronomy.

3. Jesus Christ said His words are life and spirit; the words of satan are also spirit, except they are of death rather than life. Some verbal proclamations carry no power and authority because the proclaimer has no significant spiritual standing. Some people can proclaim curses that have weight of unseen authority with them, yet other people could repeat the exact same words and they would be empty.

EXERCISES

A. Study Deuteronomy 28:15-19; how can you be certain to avoid curses?

Discussion

_____

_____

_____

B. Who ultimately has control over and limits curses?

Discussion

_____

_____

_____

C. Do you give Jesus' life-and-spirit words more credibility than the death-and-destroying words of the evil one?

Discussion

_____

_____

_____

❧

Can Christians be Possessed by a Demonic Spirit?

 POINTS TO NOTE

1. A born-again Christian has the Spirit of God dwelling in him or her. No evil spirit can possess the Holy Spirit living in the Christian. But the soul and body of any person, including Christians, are how the person interacts with the world. These parts are accessible to the evil spirit and can be hijacked for wicked and ungodly purposes (see Rom. 6:12-13; 12:1-2).

2. _"Do not conform any longer to the pattern of this world, but be transformed by the renewing of your mind. Then you will be able to test and approve what God's will is—His good, pleasing and perfect will_ (Rom.12:2).

3. An evil spirit can influence born-again Christians in some areas of life but never take total control.

 **EXERCISES**

A. Have you allowed any part of your body or soul to be hijacked?

Discussion

_____

_____

_____

B. Write Romans 12:2 in your own words. Write Romans 12:2 as a prayer to your heavenly Father.

Discussion

_____

_____

_____

C. Do you have a suspicion that there is an evil spirit influencing a part of you? What can you do to rid yourself of this spirit?

Discussion

_____

_____

_____

⌘

⌘ PRACTICAL PRINCIPLES AND DISCUSSION ⌘

_____

_____

_____

_____

_____

CHAPTER 7

Evil Spirits and Deliverance

 POINTS TO NOTE

The following are fourteen ways to recognize the presence and influence of an evil spirit:

- Unnatural, unreasonable, or intensively compulsive desires.

- Restlessness or persistent lack of inner peace—when everything becomes a struggle.

- Inability to concentrate on anything, chronic depression, incessant procrastination, or the feeling of a dark cloud hanging over your life.

- Recurrence of defying thoughts, ideas, or suggestions.

- A tendency for an attitude or reaction to get out of control, such as lust, sexual perversion, or anger.

- Appetites that are pervasive, out of proportion, invasive, or enslaving.

- Impatience—remember, anything that cannot wait is not of God.

- Inability to tame the tongue.

- Condemnation, doubts, low esteem, fear, insecurity, or physical torment; undue feelings of being trapped, abandoned, or betrayed.

- A tendency to unnecessary compromise on spiritual issues.

- Marriage problems that run in the family no matter what; for example, the inability to attain family unity, peace.

- When insufficiency or the spirits of poverty run a family, despite some members earning a high wage or income.

- Repeated incidence of premature deaths in the family.

- When parental dishonor runs in the family.

 **EXERCISES**

A. Does this list help you identify evil spirits that may be affecting you or your family?

Discussion

_____

_____

_____

B. Out of the fourteen symptoms listed, did any especially seem to ring true in your life?

Discussion

_____

_____

_____

C. Do know what to do to rid yourself of these evil spirits?

Discussion

_____

_____

_____

Understanding Demon Workings

 POINTS TO NOTE

The following 10 ways are how demons work:

- They are earth-bound.

- They have personalities; hence, they have names, and they can see, feel, and reason. Also, they drive, push, or compel their victims.

- They are self-conscious and often very knowledgeable. The sons of Sceva had more than they bargained for when they met with knowledgeable demons (see Acts 19:13-16a).

- They need homes, as they are disembodied spirits (see Matt. 12:43-45a). They have memories, can assess, work in unity, and have a sense of territorial domain.

- They operate a highly organized structure of orders and ranks (see Mark 9:28-29). Some leave by simple praying, and others go by prayer and fasting, which is reflective of their ranks.

- They are capable of taking control of certain areas of one's life, but rarely do they take total control of a person. The story of the demoniac of Gerasenes illustrates a person that was totally taken over by the demons (see Mark 5:1-13).

- They have desire and can make decisions— *"I will return to the house I left."*

- They are cast out by the Word of God (see Matt. 8:14-16).

- They believe there is one God: *"You believe that there is one God. Good! Even the demons believe that—and shudder"* (James 2:19).

- They are not omnipresent, not omniscient, nor omnipotent.

 EXERCISES

A. Were any of the ways listed a surprise to you? Which one(s) and why?

Discussion

_____

_____

_____

B. If demons are cast out by the Word of God, why don't all people use the Word to maintain spiritual freedom?

Discussion

_____

_____

_____

C. Do you sometimes give evil more credibility than God's Word? Do you sometimes feel that evil is more overwhelming that God's love?

Discussion

_____

_____

_____

The Dynamics of Deliverance

 POINTS TO NOTE

1. Deliverance covers a spectrum of activities, ranging from the seemingly small but important constant rebuking and rebuffing of the attempts of the devil to influence our lives, to the hard and difficult expulsion of a deeply seated and powerful demon that leaves only by "fasting and prayers."

2. Any Holy Spirit-filled believer can minister deliverance, or you can conduct a personal deliverance. Either way, these three important points must be fulfilled: You must have faith in the atoning blood of Jesus Christ to tap into the blessing from it. You must submit to the application and supremacy of the Word of God—demons are cast out by the spoken Word of God. You must believe in the authority of the deliverance minister, or in the case of personal deliverance, in your ability to conduct the deliverance—have faith.

3. *Key Steps in Deliverance:* Forgiveness, repentance, and prayerfulness are vital tools in deliverance. Be sensitive in the spirit to discern what spirit is being confronted. Evil spirits have personalities and are very self-conscious. Demons are cast out by spoken words (see Matt. 8:14-16). The laying on of hands is not particularly specified in Scripture as being necessary for deliverance—an inexperienced person should avoid laying on of hands before the demon is actually cast out. Dialoguing with demons should be left in the hands of an experienced person; demons may be very knowledgeable and might prove difficult for the inexperienced.

4. Internalized evil spirits may return to where they have been driven from—it is vital that you learn how to block the entry points by crucifying the flesh. Flesh is the soul (mind, emotion, and will) and is not ruled by the Spirit of God. To maintain your deliverance, you must guard your mind, emotion, and will with all diligence (see 2 Cor. 13:5).

 EXERCISES

A. How experienced are you are rebuking and rebuffing evil spirits? At fasting and praying?

Discussion

_____

_____

_____

B. Deliverance is an ongoing process in life. When you discern the crouching influence of an evil spirit at your door, do you cast it out?

Discussion

_____

_____

_____

C. Do you regularly and sincerely make forgiveness, repentance, and prayer part of your daily lifestyle? Are you spiritually sensitive in your routine throughout the day?

Discussion

_____

_____

_____

Planned Prayer for Reversing Curses

POINTS TO NOTE

The following are nine steps to take to reverse curses:

- Look for Bible passage(s) relevant to the issue and pray these to God (see Col. 2:14-15 KJV; Gal. 3:13; Num. 23:23; 2 Tim. 4:18).

- Confess any sins that have given the enemy a legal right to place a curse on the bloodline.

- Repent and ask God for forgiveness and cleansing.

- Command all curses against you to be broken in the name of Jesus.

- Take authority over inherited curses and command them to be broken.

- Take authority over curses emanating from: living in a cursed land; handling cursed objects; witchcraft curses; your old life.

- Cancel the repercussions of all curses.

- Take authority over any curses unknown to you and break them.

- Ask the power of the Holy Spirit to render any negative speech and invited curses against you as powerless.

EXERCISES

A. Do you feel empowered knowing the steps to take to reverse curses and recognize evil spirits?

Discussion

_____

_____

_____

❧

PRACTICAL PRINCIPLES AND DISCUSSION

CHAPTER 8

Blessings

Opposite Forces to Curses

 POINTS TO NOTE

1. A curse is a pronouncement or sentence of condemnation or judgment, programmed to bring about limitation on a target. On the other hand a *blessing* is a pronouncement of an approval, encouragement, divine favor, or gift from God, to succeed (see Rom. 11:29 AMP).

2. Blessings are more valuable than money, stronger than any earthly power, and surpass any manner of learning. They are divine enablings to achieve success. *A blessing can cancel a curse, but a curse cannot cancel a blessing* because a curse can be reversed, but a divine blessing is irrevocable.

3. If a blessing is not used for God's purposes, it will become futile. An example of this can be found in the blessing to make money. If care is not taken in its proper use, it could be cursed by "holes in the pockets." Though such a blessing to make money stands, the eventual outcome becomes an exercise in futility.

 EXERCISES

A. List all of the blessings you have received from God during the past week. Don't forget the air that you breathe and the peace in your heart.

Discussion

_____

_____

_____

B. Now realize that for every blessing you have received, each one can cancel any and all curses that may be limiting your supernatural lifestyle. Do you believe that truth?

Discussion

_____

_____

_____

C. re you using all of your God-given blessings for His purposes, plans, and will for your life?

Discussion

_____

_____

_____

∾⌒∾⌒∾

Breaking Curses

POINTS TO NOTE

1. The highest blessing or deliverance is the blessing in the atoning blood of Christ. This power is greater than any force that the enemy can muster. The Bible says, *"And everyone who calls on the name of the Lord will be saved"* (Joel 2:32a). Your deliverance started when you accepted Jesus Christ as your personal Savior.

2. A curse or a blessing hangs in the air until we allow it to alight. We must recognize the interchangeable principle of blessings and curses and deliberately choose blessing and life. You must also get rid of accursed things in your midst. A curse can come to rest on inanimate objects or animals, which then become accursed (see Joshua 7:13 NKJV).

3. To break a curse involves repentance to appropriate the mercy of God—mercy is the exception from judgment or punishment. It tackles the spiritual existence of the curse and blocks the loophole that the evil agent who polices the curse may use to gain entrance again.

EXERCISES

A. Do truly believe and solely rely on the promise in Joel 2:32 that you will be saved when you call on the name of the Lord?

Discussion

_____

_____

_____

B. To attract blessings rather than curses that are in the air surrounding you, have you destroyed anything that may be accursed?

Discussion

_____

_____

_____

C. Is repentance and forgiveness part of your daily communication with God? Why or why not?

Discussion

_____

_____

_____

∽∾∽

∾ PRACTICAL PRINCIPLES AND DISCUSSION ∾

_____

_____

_____

_____

_____

_____

_____

_____

_____

_____

CHAPTER 9

Assessing Your Blessings

 POINTS TO NOTE

1. God wants us to have life abundantly and flourish in our divine blessings, but the devil wants to deny us of these divine blessings and plunder our inheritance on earth. He wants to destroy the dominion that God has given to us on the earth. Consequently, when we pull divine blessings from the spirit realm into the realities of our lives, we tilt the balance toward the plans and purposes of God, bringing the justice of God into the realities of our lives.

2. Fulfillment of any divine promise belongs to God. But it is our responsibility to work that process toward its fulfillment. If we work the process, we hasten the fulfillment, and if we renege on the process, we delay or hinder or even cancel the promise.

3. Revelations often show us the blessings that exist in the heavenly realm and prompt us to their availability in the heavenly realm. Blessings are more important and valuable than money, stronger than any earthly power, and surpass any manner of learning; we should work them into our lives. Blessings are the empowerment to achieve success, a divine enabling to achieve success.

 EXERCISES

A. When you pull divine blessings from the spirit realm into your life, you tilt the balance toward the plans and purposes of God, bringing the justice of God into reality. Are you ready to pull?

Discussion

_____

_____

_____

B. Are you working the process and hasten the fulfillment of blessing? Or are you reneging, delaying, hindering, or even cancelling the promise?

Discussion

_____

_____

_____

C. Are you firmly convinced that blessings are more important and valuable than money, stronger than any earthly power, and surpass any manner of learning?

Discussion

_____

_____

_____

∽∝∾

Receiving Blessings

 POINTS TO NOTE

1. The first thing to do in preparing to receive our blessings is to ensure that every negative stronghold in our lives is eliminated. Negative strongholds are the landing pads for curses and are major hindrances to the pulling down of our blessings. Negative strongholds include fears, bitterness, jealousy, unforgiveness, anger, or covetousness (see 2 Cor. 10:4).

2. Likewise, obedience to God, a willing heart, and a life surrendered to Jesus Christ are the landing pads of blessings in our lives. _"Come now, let us reason together," says the Lord. "Though your sins are like scarlet, they shall be as white as snow; though they are red as crimson, they shall be like wool._ **_If you are willing and obedient, you will eat the best from the land_** (Isa. 1:18-19).

3. Genesis 1:28 (AMP) is a prophetic blessing of special empowerment enabling us to prevail even in difficult circumstances—through redemption by the blood of Jesus Christ. We can take dominion over any insurrection of the enemy, which could manifest as impending or present danger in our lives as we walk with God.

 **EXERCISES**

A. Are there any negative strongholds—fears, bitterness, jealousy, unforgiveness, anger, covetousness—lurking somewhere within you?

Discussion

_____

_____

_____

B. Obedience to God, a willing heart, and a life surrendered to Jesus Christ are the landing pads of blessings in your life. Are your landing pads ready to receive?

Discussion

_____

_____

_____

C. *"Be fruitful, multiply, and fill the earth, and subdue it, using all its vast resources in the service of God and man; and have dominion over the fish of the sea, the birds of the air, and over every living creature that moves upon the earth"* (Genesis 1:28 AMP). Write this verse in your own words after prayerful meditation.

Discussion

_____

_____

_____

_____

_____

Activation of Promises and Blessings

 POINTS TO NOTE

1. Activation of promises and blessings usually begins with verbal declaration of the inspired words. Always wait for the prompting of the Holy Spirit and His *rhema*. The first thing in the process of activation is to give voice to the promises of God in our lives by declaring them to the hearing the witnesses in the natural realm.

2. The process of activation involves:

- Simple things of our thought process or the power of holy imagination of seeing the promises of God by the eye of faith while yet in the invisible realm.

- Embracing the promise and meditating or pondering on it.

- Confessing, because through our prophetic confession or proclamation on earth, the angels are enabled to battle the forces of darkness, particularly when the confession lines up with the will of God.

3. The Scripture is full of examples of what other people did to pull down their blessings, and what we should emulate. We should have Abraham's kind of faith (see Rom. 4:18-22). We should have Moses' kind of commitment (see Heb. 11:24-27). Job's kind of integrity (see Job 19:25). We should act on what is revealed (see Deut. 29:29). We should keep the prophetic message (see 1 Tim. 1:18-19). We should believe the prophecies given to us (see 2 Chron. 20:20b NKJV). We should meditate on the words of God (see Josh. 1:8).

 EXERCISES

A. After waiting for the prompting of the Holy Spirit and His *rhema*, do you give voice to the promises of God in your life by declaring them to witnesses in the natural realm?

Discussion

_____

_____

_____

B. To activate your blessings and promises, do you use your eye of faith to "see" them? Do you embrace them as if you already have them? Do you proclaim their existence?

Discussion

_____

_____

_____

C. Which examples do you tend to emulate the most? The least? Why?

Discussion

_____

_____

_____

∽ PRACTICAL PRINCIPLES AND DISCUSSION ∽

CHAPTER 10

Regaining the Desolate Inheritance

 POINTS TO NOTE

1. A *desolate inheritance* is the blessing or gifting that has *lapsed into idleness* or disuse or any other forms of waste or abandonment. Desolation of an inheritance could be as a result of generational lapse or judgmental suspension from the rights and benefits of the blessing or inheritance.

2. There are two types of desolate inheritance.

> • When an inheritance or blessing has not been used in the natural realm and has not been used by the past generation, it still exists in the realm of the spirit. The most common cause of this type of desolation is lack of the knowledge of the Triune God, even though great giftedness exists in the family. Most often the process involves redemption by the blood of Jesus Christ (salvation). As exemplified by the first man; Adam brought the curse upon humankind and Jesus broke the curse and replaced it with blessing for those redeemed by His blood.
>
> • When the inheritance or blessing has been walked in by someone in the past generation but has fallen into disuse thereafter. In most cases even certain levels of spiritual maturity may have been attained in the use of the gift. This type of desolate inheritance can be regained, and the family can move in an accelerated pace toward the already acquired level of spiritual maturity that existed in the previous generation.

3. Biblical passages relevant to this principle of transference of blessings or curses through the generation include Romans 5:15-19 and Hebrews 7:6-10.

EXERCISES

A. Is it possible that within your family tree a blessing or gifting has lapsed into idleness or disuse or any other forms of waste or abandonment?

Discussion

_____

_____

_____

B. Describe in your own words the two types of desolate inheritance.

Discussion

_____

_____

_____

C. Jesus was the ultimate gift of righteousness and provision of grace—how does this statement relate to desolate inheritance?

Discussion

_____

_____

_____

ᏣᎠᏨᎠ

Five Steps to Claim your Desolate Inheritance

 POINTS TO NOTE

1. Seek details about any blessing that has become desolate; ask God for His will regarding the blessing and plead that He might use you (see Judges 13:12-13). God visited the family of Manoah with a promise to end the desolation of Israel; the family rightly requested the rules of life for entering into that inheritance.

2. Find the reason for the desolation, then repent, purify, and sanctify yourself and others in readiness. Make appropriate restitution (see Dan. 9:1-3). In Daniel's bid to recover Israel's desolate inheritance, he:

    •   Made an intensive search for the reason for the desolation.

- Discovered the reason for the desolation and the extent of the desolation, together with the magnitude of the prescribed punishment.

- Humbled himself in prayers and fasting.

- Confessed the sins of his ancestors and also for his generation.

3. Equip yourself and others for the specific assignment connected to the blessing. When King Hezekiah discovered the desolation of his people, he carried out purification, sanctification, and consecration of the temple and the priesthood and proclaimed a Passover (see 2 Chron. 29:3-11, 29-30).

4. Ensure there are no compromises in fulfilling the plans of God. Joshua did not completely eradicate the remnant of the Gath tribe as prescribed by God and that mistake later became a reproach to the nation of Israel (see Josh. 11:22). Out of this small remnant came Goliath (see 1 Sam. 17:4-11). See also Judges 11:23-24, First Kings 21:3, Joshua 11:23.

5. Make commitment by public declaration for righteousness as you walk with God regarding the possession of the blessing (see Deut. 11:29). When you make pronouncements publicly, what you say will be witnessed by a great cloud of witnesses in the spirit realm.

 EXERCISES

A. Are you willing to take the five steps to claim your desolate inheritance?

Discussion

_____

_____

_____

B. Are you ready to search for any and all details about any desolate blessing, asking God for His will and pleading for Him to use you?

Discussion

_____

_____

_____

C. Are you equipped to receive the desolate inheritance on behalf of yourself and your generation?

Discussion

_____

_____

_____

∼ PRACTICAL PRINCIPLES AND DISCUSSION ∼

CHAPTER 11

Holy Spirit and The Anointing

 ## POINTS TO NOTE

1. It is important to distinguish the person of the Holy Spirit, who is the giver of the anointing, and the anointing itself. The anointing is not synonymous with the Person of the Holy Spirit; it is possible to operate in the anointing, which is a gift and therefore irrevocable, without the presence of the Holy Spirit.

2. We are never alone; He lives in us. Though the Holy Spirit is omnipresent, He is not "omni-body." This means He does not live in everybody but dwells only in believers (see John 14:15-17).

3. Though invisible as a spirit, the Holy Spirit has all the attributes of a personality (except, of course, the frailty and sinfulness of humankind). There are numerous instances in Scripture where the Holy Spirit is personified. The personality of the Holy Spirit is mentioned in John 16:7-8; Romans 8:26; Isaiah 63:10a; Ephesians 4:30; Acts 5:3; 1 Corinthians 12:11; and Romans 8:14 NKJV.

 ## EXERCISES

A. What is the difference between the Holy Spirit and the Anointing that He gives believers?

Discussion

_____

_____

_____

B. Are you aware of the Holy Spirit's presence living within you?

Discussion

_____

_____

_____

C. How many personality traits can you list from reading the Scriptures mentioned?

Discussion

_____

_____

_____

༈

The Deity of the Holy Spirit

 POINTS TO NOTE

1. The Holy Spirit is not just a personality; He is God. The deity of the Holy Spirit is evident from Him as Creator, all powerful, omnipresent, omniscient, and eternal (see Gen. 1:1-2; Job 33:4; Micah 3:8; Job 42:2; Luke 1:35a; Ps. 139:7-10; 1 Cor. 2:10; Heb. 9:14).

EXERCISES

A. Is "deity" a clear or confusing word to define? What does the deity of God mean to you? What Scriptures define it for you?

Discussion

_____

_____

_____

Recognizing the Holy Spirit Prompting

POINTS TO NOTE

1. *Conscience* is recognizing between right and wrong regarding your conduct. Conscience is a natural instinct, even for those not filled with the Holy Spirit (see Titus 1:15). However, if we are filled with the Holy Spirit, our conscience becomes sanctified (see Heb. 9:14).

2. Willful sin is the persistent rebellion against the prompting of the Holy Spirit. Psalm 19:13 says, *"Keep your servant also from willful sins; may they not rule over me. Then will I be blameless, innocent of great transgression."*

3. One of the greatest obstacles in recognizing the voice of the Holy Spirit is the voice of your mind. The world plays out with resonating logic and reasoning in your mind, but the voice of faith by which you can please God is quiet, gentle, peaceful, and not forceful (see 1 Kings 19:11-12).

 EXERCISES

A. Do you more often than not listen to your conscience when faced with a right or wrong situation? How attuned are you to your conscience?

Discussion

_____

_____

_____

B. Do you persistently rebel against the Holy Spirit's prompting?

Discussion

_____

_____

_____

C. Are you listening to your voice of faith, the voice of the Holy Spirit, or the voices of the world?

Discussion

_____

_____

_____

༄

Knowing the Works of the Holy Spirit

1. The gifts of the Spirit revealed in First Corinthians 12:4-11 are supernatural abilities that are imparted by the Holy Spirit for the purpose equipping the saints with power for service.

2. Baptism in the Holy Spirit came upon the disciples with power, as a mighty rushing wind that transformed ordinary people to those with supernatural abilities (see Acts 2:1-4)

3. To experience the baptism of the Holy Spirit, you must come to Jesus Christ in truth and in Spirit as the disciples did; come to Him thirsty for the Spirit; come to Him seeking cleansing; come to Him expecting and while worshiping in the right environment.

 EXERCISES

A. List the gifts of the Spirit found in First Corinthians 12:4-11. With which gift or gifts has the Lord blessed you?

Discussion

_____

_____

_____

B. Have you experience the baptism in the Holy Spirit? What manifestations were present?

Discussion

_____

_____

_____

❧❧❧

❧ PRACTICAL PRINCIPLES AND DISCUSSION ❧

_____

_____

_____

_____

_____

_____

_____

CHAPTER 12

The Anointing

 POINTS TO NOTE

1. Anointing is the setting apart or consecration for a divine function. It is the transference of divine power to enable the person to carry out a specified function. It originates from God and is given by His Spirit. In the spirit realm, anointing starts from the verbal proclamation of God.

2. In the physical realm, anointing is symbolized by the pouring oil on the head of the one to be anointed or on the object to be consecrated. Applying oil in the Old Testament is equivalent to baptism in the New Testament—it is the outward sign of inward grace.

3. A believer grows and matures in the anointing before eventually walking in it. You cannot live a spiritually supernatural life by anointing only; you need character to carry it. Most of the time the anointing is concealed before the time of its manifestation, and you can be anointed without realizing it, just like Jeremiah (see Jer. 1:4-10).

 EXERCISES

A. Have you witnessed someone receiving God's anointing to carry out a specific duty or function that furthers His Kingdom?

Discussion

_____

_____

_____

B. Does your church pastor or ministry leader anoint people with oil? Under what circumstances?

Discussion

_____

_____

_____

C. Do you believe you are mature enough to walk in your anointing? Why or why not?

Discussion

_____

_____

_____

Growing and Maturing in the Anointing

 POINTS TO NOTE

1. Factors that cause the anointing to grow:

> • Faithfulness to the things of God.
>
> • Submission to God—in the authority that God has placed over you.
>
> • Sacrifice—laying aside personal agenda, preferring the interest of others and God to self-interest.
>
> • Spending time with God—growing in intimacy that will intimidate the enemy.
>
> • Growing in the Word of God.
>
> • Growing in the power of the Lord.
>
> • Dealing with things within us such as dying to self.
>
> • Respecting the anointing in others ahead of us.
>
> • The role of spiritual authority over us in the helping or hindering to bring one to maturity.

2. Whenever God anoints a person, it occurs with power to protect, to preserve, and to guide. However, the effectiveness of the anointing at the point of expression is influenced by important factors such as the *place* and the *time* of expression. The place of the anointing and the time of anointing must come together in maturity

3. Anointing is given to a person in order to reach out to a specific group of people. For example, Peter was the apostle to the Jews, and Paul was the apostle to the Gentiles. Even Jesus Christ said He was sent only to *"the lost sheep of Israel"* (Matt. 15:24) before His resurrection, although salvation became available to Gentiles after His death and resurrection.

EXERCISES

A. How many factors are working in your life right now causing the anointing to grow?

Discussion

_____

_____

_____

B. Do you feel empowered to protect, to preserve, and to guide? Or is your anointing still maturing—as it took Joseph many years to fully into his anointed destiny.

Discussion

_____

_____

_____

C. Have you been anointed to reach out to a certain people group? Who and why?

Discussion

_____

_____

_____

༄

Wasted and Corporate Anointing

 POINTS TO NOTE

1. Many people have wasted the anointing of God in their lives. A biblical example of this is found in Ezekiel 28:14-17). Anointing can also diminish without notice, as seen in the life of Samson (see Judges 16:17-20). Many people are operating in the emptiness of what used to be the glory of yesterday. If they will only humble themselves, then they will be restored (see Judg. 16:28). The periodic intensification of anointing is also sometimes required (see 2 Kings 3:15-16).

2. Individual anointing can be harnessed into corporate anointing, as there are also certain levels of spiritual resistance that we cannot overcome without corporate unity (see Exod. 17:8-16).

3. The characteristics of anointing are: transferable; subject to renewal; increases; decreases; may occur on and off; originates from the Holy Spirit but works differently in different people.

 EXERCISES

A. Can you think of people who may be wasting their anointing? Are you one of them?

Discussion

_____

_____

_____

B. Can you think of a modern-day example of a time when individual anointing was harnessed into corporate anointing?

Discussion

_____

_____

_____

C. Does knowing the characteristics of anointing help you recognize the importance of God's anointing in your life?

Discussion

_____

_____

_____

❧ PRACTICAL PRINCIPLES AND DISCUSSION ❧

CHAPTER 13

The Prophetic

 POINTS TO NOTE

1. Any statement from God that speaks of something that will happen in the future is called prophecy. Prophecy originates from intimacy with God and speaks of His relationship with humankind—revealing the heart of God, speaking the truth of God, and doing so in love (see 1 Pet. 4:11).

2. Prophecy is not all about predicting future events; God also informs, directs, teaches, encourages, and builds up the Body of Christ through prophecy. God calls believers to respond appropriately on earth to what He is doing in Heaven.

3. The Word of God was written because men of old were inspired by the Spirit of God. Genesis to Revelation was written by prophets or is about prophecy (see Heb. 1:1-2a).

 EXERCISES

A. Are you intimate enough with God to receive the gift of prophecy—to reveal His heart to other believers?

Discussion

_____

_____

_____

B. What type(s) of prophecy have you witnessed? Experienced?

Discussion

_____

_____

_____

C. Do you have a favorite biblical prophet of old? A modern-day prophet?

Discussion

_____

_____

_____

Word of Knowledge

 POINTS TO NOTE

1. Word of knowledge is a gift of the Holy Spirit that lets you know something beyond the natural means through God's revelation. *"To one there is given through the Spirit the message of wisdom, to another the message of knowledge by means of the same Spirit"* (1 Cor. 12:8). It speaks of the past or the present, but never the future.

2. Points to remember in differentiating between word of knowledge from true and false prophets:

> - Word of knowledge from a true prophet has divine power to heal, break mindsets, restore and bring liberty.
>
> - Word of knowledge from a false prophet is lacking in divine power, has no healing or restoration, and drives the victim toward hatred, bitterness, or vengeance.
>
> - Word of knowledge from a true prophet should be followed either by a prophetic word or by immediate deliverance from the identified bondage.
>
> - Word of knowledge from a false prophet is not followed by prophetic word or divine intervention in the situation; an empty confirmation of what is known.
>
> - Word of knowledge from a false prophet creates sensationalism; does not draw attention to the love and grace of God.

EXERCISES

A. Has God ever given you a word of knowledge to share with someone? Has someone ever shared a word of knowledge from God to you?

Discussion

_____

_____

_____

B. How easy do you think it will be to tell the difference between a word of knowledge and true and false prophets?

Discussion

_____

_____

_____

☙❧

The Flow of Prophecy

 POINTS TO NOTE

1. Prophecy should originate from the Lord and not from human imagination. We see this in Second Peter 1:21.

2. The Holy Spirit equips the prophet with the required revelation about the situation. Examining Ezekiel 37:1-14 we see that:

   - The first thing the prophet receives is revelation that is for information only. _"Set me in the middle of a valley; it was full of bones."_

   - There is then a process of acquiring detailed insight about the revelation. _"He led me back and forth among them, and I saw a great many dry bones on the floor of the valley, bones that were very dry."_

   - This is followed by a period of dialoguing. _"He asked me, 'Son of man, can these bones live?'"_ In particular, the prophet should ask what to do with the revelation received. _"O Sovereign Lord, You alone know."_

- Then speak life, not death; prophecy literally means bringing forth. *"Prophesy to these bones...I will make breath enter you, and you will come to life."*

- The prophet should not be deterred by the apparent deadness of the situation. *"The bones were very dry."*

- You should be alert and remain watchful and sensitive in the spirit. *"As I was prophesying, there was a noise, a rattling sound, and the bones came together.... I looked, and tendons and flesh appeared on them."*

- The prophetic word is like a seed that needs to be nurtured even if it means giving another prophecy to reinforce the previous one. *"But there was no breath in them. Then He said to me, 'Prophesy to the breath...Come from the four winds, O breath, and breathe into these slain, that they may live.'"* It progressively unfolds with time until it is fulfilled.

- Wait for the interpretation. This is the part that many find difficult. Most people miss it at this stage and end up in error, even though they have seen correctly. It is God that gives interpretation. *"Then He told me what the vision meant"* (Ezek. 37:11 LB).

- The vision was interpreted by God: *Then He said to me: "Son of man, these bones are the house of Israel ...declares the Lord'"* (Ezek. 37:11-14).

 EXERCISES

A. *"For prophecy never had its origin in the will of man, but men spoke from God as they were carried along by the Holy Spirit."* Have you witnessed someone speaking as if from God but the word actually came from the person's own imagination? What was the effect on the hearer(s)?

Discussion

_____

_____

_____

B. Does God always equip a prophet with the required revelation about the situation?

Discussion

_____

_____

_____

❧

PRACTICAL PRINCIPLES AND DISCUSSION

CHAPTER 14

Beginner's Guide to Prophecy

 POINTS TO NOTE

1. The way a prophet comes across to people is as important as the content of his or her message. There is always a human component to prophesying. Your personality will affect the way you see things, therefore affecting the way you deliver prophecy. Extroverts tend to exaggerate while introverts tend to be conservative: *"The spirits of prophets are subject to the control of prophets"* (1 Cor. 14:32). Revelation is a product of your relationship with God.

2. Some people are seers, some are hearers, others just move in faith, and many get prophetic utterances by feeling (spiritual discernment). Here are some guidelines to prophesying:

    *   After divine inspiration has been received, the prophet should start with the obvious.

    *   Ask the Holy Spirit questions. He responds to faith, trust, peace, and the expectancy of our spirit.

    *   Recall previous knowledge. God uses "mental imprints" born out of your experience to speak to you.

    *   Do not spiritualize everything. An everyday event should assume prophetic significance only if a quickening in the spirit prompts it.

    *   Avoid rationalization. The closer the prophetic word is to what you have received, the more accurate the prophecy is. Use words like, "I see a picture; I think it means…" rather than "Thus says the Lord."

    *   Allow for the test of time. A prophetic word is a seed. It needs to be nurtured and watered in order to grow (see Ps. 105:19 NKJV).

    *   Do not add to what you have received, either out of sheer enthusiasm or eagerness to impress. You do not have the full picture; the prophet knows in parts and prophecy comes in parts (see 1 Cor. 13:9; Deut. 29:29).

    *   All personal prophecies are conditional and unfold progressively over a lifetime. Stay away from those who give personal prophecies but who would not like to be quoted.

    *   Here are some conditions that stir up the prophetic: High praise and worship (see 2 Kings 3:15 NKJV); the company of other prophets (see 1 Sam. 10:10); when hands are laid on a person (see Acts 19:6).

    *   The word of God is the fountain of life for the prophetic: see 1 Samuel 3:7,21; 4:1a). Samuel's word came to Israel only after he knew the word of God.

EXERCISES

A. Did you ever consider that your (or a prophet's) personality will affect the way you see things, therefore affecting the way you deliver prophecy?

Discussion

_____

_____

_____

B. Of the guidelines listed, which two should you concentrate on most to ensure an accurate prophecy?

Discussion

_____

_____

_____

❧❧❧

Responding to and Judging Prophecy

 POINTS TO NOTE

1. The most important thing to do after receiving a personal prophecy is to make yourself available to God in prayerful submission. Do not rush into any major decision unless the prophecy specifically says to. The how and when of the fulfillment belongs to God. He who promises is well able to fulfill that which He has said.

2. Many prophetic promises have failed because the one who heard them has failed to understand, interpret correctly, obey, respond appropriately, wait upon, or act upon them at the right time. See First Corinthians 13:8 (NKJV) and First Thessalonians 5:19-21.

3. Test the following (see 1 John 4:1):

   - The spirit of the prophecy.
   - The content of the prophecy.
   - The fruit of the prophecy.
   - The prophet.

Ask the following of the *spirit* of the prophecy:

> - Is it the spirit of God?
> - Is it the spirit of man?
> - Is it a combination of the two listed above?
> - Is it the spirit of the devil?

4. Also ask the following questions about the *content* of the prophecy:

> - Does it line up with the Scriptures?
> - Does it flow against God's love?
> - Does it have divine power? True prophecy has enough divine power to bring encouragement and inner conviction to turn people away from sin.
> - Does it bring you closer to God?
> - Is it overbearing?

To discern the *spirit* behind the prophecy, the following points are crucial to remember:

> - The Holy Spirit does not control but fills you and requires your cooperation.
> - The demonic spirit will control without cooperation, permission, or mercy. Demonic control wants to be total and does not give choice.
> - The human spirit is able to control through mental manipulation.
> - The Holy Spirit leads you by guidance, but a demonic spirit pushes.

Ask the following questions of the *spirit*:

> - Does it seek to control?
> - Is it gentle or forceful?
> - Does it lack real content? If it is negative, then it is always bad news, leaving people hollow and empty, or filled with fear.
> - Is it a cause of division within the fellowship?
> - Is it judgmental?

Here are some points on the *fruit* of *true* prophecy:

> • It brings life.
>
> • It gives spiritual vision—hope, encouragement, and faith.
>
> • It edifies, exhorts, and comforts.
>
> • It brings revival and restoration to God.
>
> • It guides you to your right place in God.

On the other hand, here are points on the fruit of *false* prophecy:

> • It causes division.
>
> • It releases fear, not faith.
>
> • It arms some factions.
>
> • It results in control and manipulation.
>
> • It produces flattery and not prophecies.
>
> • It makes people indebted to the minister

 EXERCISES

A. What is the most important thing to do after receiving a personal prophecy? Should you rush into any major decision? Who does the fulfillment belong to? Has He promised to fulfill His word to you?

Discussion

_____

_____

_____

B. *"Dear friends, do not believe every spirit, but **test the spirits** to see whether they are from God, because many false prophets have gone out into the world"* (1 John 4:1). How important is it to test the spirits? Are you gullible, believing whatever a person tells you?

Discussion

_____

_____

_____

C. Are you going to take the Bible's advice and test the spirit of the prophecy, content of the prophecy, fruit of the prophecy, and the prophet?

Discussion

_____

_____

_____

∽↝↜∾

Beware of False Prophets

POINTS TO NOTE

1. False prophets use their gifts and other people to build their own influence or ministry. Most times, a prophet's quality of life and motivations show if he or she is a true or false prophet. A proven track record of true and accurate prophecies establishes a prophet.

2. A false prophet falls into one of two categories: When he or she knowingly moves on a consistent basis without the inspiration of God and with a mind to deceive. When a gifted prophet uses his or her gift for personal gain, influence, and the building of personal ministry. Both of these ways will draw people away from God. The prophet Moses made a profound statement that relates to this in Numbers 11:29.

3. The characteristics of false prophets include: unscriptural utterances (see 2 Tim. 4:3-5); motivated by monetary gain (see Titus 1:10-11); talk of fleshly or carnal desires and are morally corrupt (see 2 Pet. 2:18-19); no spiritual power in lives or ministry because truth is mixed with error (see 2 John 10); dangerous because they are very persuasive (see Acts 20:28-31).

EXERCISES

A. Do you always look for a prophet's motives and track record before believing what is being said? Do you sometimes? Almost never?

Discussion

_____

_____

_____

B. Have you ever met or been in the presence of a false prophet who fell into one of the two categories mentioned? Did the so-called prophet have a following? Why do you think people follow false prophets?

Discussion

_____

_____

_____

C. To deceive a person, does a false prophet have to exhibit all of the characteristics mentioned or only a few? Only one?

Discussion

_____

_____

_____

❧

❧ PRACTICAL PRINCIPLES AND DISCUSSION ❧

_____

_____

_____

_____

_____

_____

_____

_____

_____

_____

_____

CHAPTER 15

Minding God's Idea

 POINTS TO NOTE

1. The mind of Christ that is in us is where God plants His ideas or thoughts or impressions, which are often characteristically gentle, peaceful, consistent, and persistent. The peace of God that rules our mind helps us know what is of God and what is not (see Phil. 4:6-7).

2. Underpinning all our spirituality is the need to recognize and appreciate the pivotal role of the human mind in divine communication. Life is about the choices we make. Most decisions of our everyday life should be predicated on recognizing divine nodding in the realm of the mind. The only problem with this is that such nodding or prompting often comes as though it were human thoughts, and may not be immediately apparent as divine.

3. Many people have missed divine guidance in their lives because they did not recognize the subtle divine prompting but sought after the spectacular. The Bible says, *In his heart a man plans his course, but the Lord determines his steps* (Proverbs 16:9). This scripture refers to a balanced and trained mind that flows in harmony with divine prompting unconsciously.

 EXERCISES

A. Are your thoughts and impressions usually gentle, peaceful, consistent, and persistent, imitating the peace of God in your mind?

Discussion

_____

_____

_____

B. Can you recognize the difference between your own noddings and promptings and those that are divine?

Discussion

_____

_____

_____

C. Do you plan your course but give the Lord free reign to direct your steps?

Discussion

_____

_____

_____

⤮

The Mind

POINTS TO NOTE

1. The mind is a silent battlefield. Even when on the surface everything seems calm and peaceful, behind the exterior the mind could be a flaming inferno with the struggles of the events and circumstances that have come across our path in life. Inner struggles or bottled-up emotions not vented leads to perversion. Whoever wins the battle of the mind wins the battle of life. I have come to the inevitable conclusion that no one can rise above the margins of his or her imagination. We must renew our mind and bring it under the rule of the spirit (see Rom. 12:2; 1 Cor. 2:14-16).

2. The mind is influenced by many sources including: the world system (see James 1:14-15); intrusion from the evil one (see 2 Cor. 4:4; 11:3); godly influences (see Rom. 12:2; Eph. 4:22-24; Acts 17:11); taking authority of your thoughts (see 2 Cor. 10:3-5). These influences impinge on the human mind in such a way that it ends up becoming one of the following: a passive mind, an unyielding mind, or a positive (balanced) mind. But we should try to have a positive mind set on the things of God.

EXERCISES

A. Have you felt as if your mind was a flaming inferno because of life's struggles? Have bottled-up emotions led to perversion and sin?

Discussion

_____

_____

_____

B. For the majority of your days, would you say you have a passive mind, an unyielding mind, or a positive (balanced) mind?

Discussion

_____

_____

_____

A Sanctified Mind

 POINTS TO NOTE

1. We live in a fallen world where things and ideas get attached to us as we travel through life. So it is necessary to continuously bring our mind to a sanctified state by:

   • Putting on the helmet of salvation to guard the thinking process (see Rom. 8:5).

   • Guarding against impure, selfish, greedy, and demeaning thoughts. Practicing the act of renewing the thought processes, means bringing basic thinking to the truth of God and turning off any ungodly thoughts.

   • Setting your mind upon the Lord (the things above only) (see Col. 3:1-2).

   • Getting your mind to dwell on godly issues and view things from a godly perspective (see Phil. 2:5 NKJV).

   • Continually reminding yourself that you have the mind of Christ.

   • Reviewing how much you consider others before yourself and how much you love God on a consistent basis.

   • Refusing to be offended, no matter what. It is inevitable that offense will come, but what counts is where you will be when the dust settles.

   • Constantly studying the Word of God. The extent to which you allow the lordship of the Word of God is the extent you have submitted to the lordship of Christ in your life.

   • Practicing holy imagination by visualizing Bible passages (see Rom. 13:14).

2. You sanctify your mind by filling your imagination with images and concepts from the Word of God or by reading and visualizing Scripture. This seasons your imagination to receive spiritual pictures in dreams and visions. The Word of God has spiritual substance so that when you submit your mind to it, the power of the Word will transform the soil of your sanctified imagination. Sanctification boosts the spirit of a sound mind, and we use the mind to appreciate and translate divine imagery into everyday routines of life.

3. The spirit of a sound mind is the divine insurance that guards against the error of presumption. It helps the delicate balancing of the human thought process so we can see things from God's perspective. It is also the security that enables us to differentiate what is of God and what is not.

 EXERCISES

A. From the list of how to bring your mind into a sanctified state, which two or three ways would you like to implement today? By the end of the month, would you like to put into practice each of the ways?

Discussion

_____

_____

_____

B. Sanctification boosts the spirit of a sound mind, and you use your mind to appreciate and translate divine imagery into everyday routines of life. How sanctified is your mind?

Discussion

_____

_____

_____

C. Sometimes there is a delicate balance act between good and evil. What tips the scale toward good? Toward evil?

Discussion

_____

_____

_____

❧ PRACTICAL PRINCIPLES AND DISCUSSION ❧

CHAPTER 16

Living Supernaturally

 POINTS TO NOTE

1. The reality is that since the fall in the Garden of Eden, we continue to live in two worlds, such that human living intersects the realm of the seen and the unseen. We can choose to live in the natural darkness of the world or we can choose to live in the *supernaturalness* of the Kingdom of God and His glorious presence.

2. Many people prefer to see the concept of spiritual and natural senses as separate; but in operative terms there is a functional continuum between the two. With proper training we should be able to slip from one to the other imperceptibly. God is Spirit, and He speaks to our spirit. Regaining Eden not only means strengthening the spiritual senses, it also requires blending the natural senses with the spiritual senses. God desires to bring humanity back to the life of intimacy with Himself that humanity once enjoyed.

 EXERCISES

C. What are the major differences of living in worldly darkness and supernatural heavenly light?

Discussion

_____

_____

_____

D. Can you easily and routinely slip from one realm to the other imperceptibly?

Discussion

_____

_____

_____

Supernatural Life in the Last Days

 POINTS TO NOTE

The following points are important regarding how to live in the supernatural in the last days:

- *Salvation:* The first step in the redemptive process is to accept Jesus Christ as your Savior (see Rev. 22:14).

- *Set Your Mind on What the Spirit Desires:* The sanctified mind is very valuable in our walk in the spirit (see Rom. 8:5).The spiritual senses and your natural senses will interact in the arena of your mind.

- *The Peace That Surpasses All Understanding:* Without peace our experience in God will be limited (see Ps. 46:10a). Peace is essential to tapping into the supernatural (see Phil. 4:4-7). Revelation comes in the stillness of your heart.

- *Hebrews 5:14 Principle:* This is exercising and maturing spiritual senses by reason of constant use. This principle applies in the natural as well as in the spiritual. Mature believers are those who, by constant exercise of their spiritual senses, are able to discriminate between sound and unsound doctrines and between wholesome and unwholesome conduct and ideas. As we obey God and step out in faith, let us do so with reverence, in the realization that by strength shall no man prevail.

- *Stepping Out in Faith:* We should avoid Gideon sign-dependency (see Judg. 6:36-40), and instead step out in faith (see Isa. 30:21).

- *Dreams and Visions:* God is bringing understanding of mysteries to us at this present age through dreams and visions. When talking about the blending of the natural and the spiritual senses as a functional continuum, see Second Corinthians 12:2.

- *Prophetic Mimicry:* This is acting out or mimicking in the natural under divine inspiration what is happening in the spiritual. It is also referred to as "prophetic acts." This will be absolutely vital in the days ahead as God will increasingly use people in prophetic acts or drama and mimicry (see Exod. 17:10-11 and 2 Kings 13:17). In the coming days, God will wake many in the middle of the night and lead them into prophetic prayer; spontaneous obedience will lead to outstanding miracles.

- *The Mantles of the Holy Spirit:* Many are going to enter a season of anointing and empowerment to operate with the mantles of the Holy Spirit. These coverings or expressions are often referred to as the seven attributes of the Spirit of God and will enable them to operate in the fullness of Christ (see Isa. 11:1-2). We are the promised generation who will do "greater works" (see John 14:12).

- *Angels on Assignments:* There will be an increase in angelic activities; many will come in concealed glory to allow interaction with humanity. Many angels are released from the heavenly realm on "conditional assignments" (assignments requiring human participation or cooperation) to bring entire missions to successful completion (see Ps. 103:20; Gen. 19:21b-22a).

- *Living the Bible Days:* Living in intense conviction and absolute trusting in the Word of God to the extent of being able to feel, and smell in your spirit the life how people lived in biblical days. This comes only through faith and intense meditation on the Word and imagery of the Bible.

- ***The Days of Heaven on Earth:*** To live in the realm of God means to be in constant communion with God the Father and the Holy Spirit—to continuously dwell in the Word of God (Jesus Christ). Through intimate fellowship with God and the Holy Spirit, it is possible to usher the heavenly perspectives into the earth. The righteous shall live by faith "That your days may be multiplied, and the days of your children, in the land which the LORD sware unto your fathers to give them, as the days of heaven upon the earth" Deut 11:21.

 EXERCISES

A. We are entering the season of manifestations of the throne room presence on earth. What does this phrase mean to you? Are you looking forward to being part of it?

Discussion

_____

_____

_____

B. In the Lord's Prayer, Jesus taught us to pray, *"Thy kingdom come. Thy will be done on earth, as it is in heaven"* (Matt. 6:10 KJV). We are living in fulfilment of this prayer. Do you believe these are *"the days of heaven upon the earth"* (Deut. 11:21b KJV), the days when the exact replica of the events and activities of the third Heaven will come upon the earth?

Discussion

_____

_____

_____

∾ PRACTICAL PRINCIPLES AND DISCUSSION ∾

PART II

Working with Angels

HOW YOU CAN LIVE AN EVERYDAY SUPERNATURAL LIFE

CHAPTER 17

Angels are Ministering Spirits

 POINTS TO NOTE

1. The angelic realm is an integral part of God's arsenal. Throughout the Bible and in the contemporary world we see the ministry intricately involved with the administration of God's purpose on earth. It was through the ministry of angels that God brought justice to the corrupt city of Sodom and Gomorrah.

2. At certain moments in time, fortunes change, history is made, and lives are affected! At these times—destiny point situations—God uses angels. Many people expect to meet angels in a stereotyped pattern. However, this is not always so. Angels do not often appear in white robes. The Bible says, *"Do not forget to entertain strangers, for by so doing some people have entertained angels without knowing it"* (Heb. 13:2).

3. Angels are involved in arranging and rearranging events and circumstances to align us to God's destiny for us. God can meet us in the most unusual place and communicate through the most unpredictable means. He manifests His will to us through diverse ways. That is why the Bible says, *"Be on the alert then, for you do not know the day nor the hour"* [of your visitation] (Matt. 25:13 NASB).

 EXERCISES

A. How familiar are you with the angelic realm?

Discussion

_____

_____

_____

B. Do you believe that God uses angels to affect history, fortunes, and destinies?

Discussion

_____

_____

_____

C. Has an angel arranged or rearranged events and circumstances to align you with God's destiny for you?

Discussion

_____

_____

_____

❧

The Multiple Roles of Angels

POINTS TO NOTE

1. The multiplicity and diversity of the angelic roles and their capabilities are often beyond the imagination of the human mind—they are involved in furthering the purpose of God on earth and in the heavenly realm. When there was a rebellion in Heaven, the archangel Michael and his angels defeated the rebels. When an evil principality withheld the divine messenger sent to Daniel, archangel Michael was dispatched to administer justice to the situation (see Dan. 10:12-14, 20-21; see also Exod. 14:19-20, Gen. 19:1-11).

2. Angels are co-servants with the saints in the service of God and are created by God for His work and also to do His pleasure. God uses angels to bring healing, salvation, comforting, even destruction and death. Angels do not do a human's bidding, as most people would want to believe, otherwise churches may have used angelic forces against each other.

3. To see angels in the physical realm is the exception rather than the rule. We walk with the angelic force by faith believing the Bible that truly they encamp around us all at all times. They are innumerable and are constantly involved in arranging and rearranging divine plans and appointments for human beings.

EXERCISES

A. In what ways can you imagine angels are involved in furthering the justice of God on earth and in the heavenly realm?

Discussion

_____

_____

_____

B. Angels do not do humans' bidding, otherwise churches may have used angelic forces against each other. What other calamities can you imagine would happen if humans could dictate to angels?

Discussion

_____

_____

_____

C. Do you daily walk with an angelic force, by faith believing they are encamped around you all at all times?

Discussion

_____

_____

_____

∾∾∾

∾ PRACTICAL PRINCIPLES AND DISCUSSION ∾

_____

_____

_____

_____

_____

_____

_____

_____

_____

_____

CHAPTER 18

The Nature of Angels

 POINTS TO NOTE

1. Angels are ministering spirits sent to help those who are heirs of salvation. They were individually created and their creation predates the creation of humankind. They are spiritual beings—superhuman in many respects—but they are not omniscient, omnipresent, or omnipotent. Angels were created from fire and winds; humans were made from the dust of the earth and became living souls by the breath of God.

2. Angels may exhibit great strength, but they are not gods and should not be worshiped. They have the capability to take on temporal appearances if their assignments warrant. Since they are to minister to heirs of salvation, their involvement in affairs of this world will be greatly increased in the end time. It is vital that we get better acquainted with and equipped to relate to angels.

3. A few characteristics, traits, and truths about angels include: Angels were created before humans (see Rev. 3:14; Job 38:4-7). Angels are part of the supernatural realm created by God (see Col. 1:16-18; Neh. 9:6). Angels are innumerable (see Heb. 12:22). Angels have limited power and knowledge (see Mark 13:32-33; Matt. 24:36; 1 Pet. 1:12; Gal. 1:8). Angels have superhuman power (see Ps. 103:20; Gen. 19:13-24; 2 Kings 19:35). Angels are everlasting; they don't procreate—they were created by God to live forever.

 EXERCISES

A. How does the creation of angels differ from the creation of humans? Why is this difference important to understand?

Discussion

_____

_____

_____

Why is it vital that you get better acquainted with and equipped to relate to angels?

Discussion

_____

_____

_____

B. Of the characteristics, traits, and truths about angels listed, did any come as a surprise to you?

Discussion

_____

_____

_____

❧

Angels' Identity and Communication

POINTS TO NOTE

1. Individual identity among angels is very restricted in the Scriptures because the focus should not be on angels but on the God who created the angels and their divine assignments. Only two holy angels are named in the Scriptures: Gabriel and Michael (see Dan. 9:21, 10:13,21; 12:1; Luke 1:19,26; Jude 9; Rev. 12:7).

2. As personalities, angels have power to communicate with one another: *"If I speak in the tongues of men and of angels, but have not love, I am only a resounding gong or a clanging cymbal"* (1 Cor. 13:1). Angels can also commune with us (see Num. 22:32-35; Acts 10:3-7).

EXERCISES

A. Do you know people who worship angels? Does current pop (or church) culture encourage this?

Discussion

_____

_____

_____

B. Has an angel ever communicated with you?

Discussion

_____

_____

_____

❧

Angel Appearances

 POINTS TO NOTE

1. Angels appear in different forms depending upon a number of things, such as:

    - Their order of creation.
    - The assignment on which they are sent.
    - The role that we are expected to play in the fulfillment of their assignment.
    - The heavenly glory in which they come to the earth.

2. The cherubim are exotic and beautiful, and they are covered with precious stones (see Ezek. 28:13-14). Seraphim are fiery angels and have six wings—with two they cover their faces, with two they cover their feet, and with two they fly. They epitomize humility and praises in the presence of God (see Isa. 6:2).

3. Appearances predicated on earthly assignments include:

    - David saw the awesome angel of the Lord at the threshing floor of Araunah.
    - Balaam saw the angel with a drawn sword.
    - Mary saw the angel Gabriel and was able to communicate with him.
    - The prophet Daniel saw the same angel as Mary but was unable to stand in his presence.

 EXERCISES

A. Did you realize that angels come in different forms? Do you find this examination of angels interesting?

    Discussion

    _____

    _____

    _____

B. After reading the descriptions of the cherubim and seraphim, do other images of angels come into your spiritually imagined mind?

    Discussion

    _____

    _____

    _____

C. Can you name other angelic appearances that were predicated on earthly assignments?

Discussion

_____

_____

_____

⌒⌒⌒

Angels and Heavenly Glory

POINTS TO NOTE

1. Occasionally angels appear with varying degrees of heavenly glory. The Bible speaks of an angel with the appearance of lightning in which reflected the degree of heavenly glory carried by that angel (see Matt. 28:1-7).

2. Gabriel appeared to Mary (see Luke 1:26:33) and the same angel Gabriel appeared with a higher level of heavenly glory—and Daniel could not even stand in his presence (see Dan. 8:15-17).

3. The amount of glory angels appear in varies according to the assignment and the degree of human interaction in the assignment. If the assignment requires interaction and discussion with humans, the glory is veiled to allow this. If the assignment is essentially for the purpose of impartation and power expression, they appear with a high degree of heavenly glory to allow for the appropriate level of authority and power to be carried from Heaven.

EXERCISES

A. *"His appearance was like lightning, and his clothes were white as snow. The guards were so afraid of him that they shook and became like dead men. The angel said to the women, 'Do not be afraid, for I know that you are looking for Jesus, who was crucified.'"* Would you be frightened if you saw an angel appearing as lightning?

Discussion

_____

_____

_____

B. It seems that Gabriel has a split personality—explain this according to Scripture and your understanding.

Discussion

_____

_____

_____

C. Why do you think God allows angels to vary their amount of glory according to their assignments with humans?

Discussion

_____

_____

_____

⌘

Angel Assignments

POINTS TO NOTE

1. *Conditional* angelic assignments require the participation of humans for completion. Therefore we need to know how to maximize our working relationship with the angels. However, most of the angels on conditional assignments also operate with provisos, as in the case of the angel that rescued Lot (see Gen. 19:18-26; also see Num. 22:31-35; Josh. 5:13-15).

2. *Unconditional* assignments are assignments that angels are to perform that are not contingent on human reaction or cooperation for completion (see Luke 1:11-13, 28-32; 1 Thess. 4:16-18).

EXERCISES

C. Which angelic assignments do you think are most common—conditional or unconditional?

Discussion

_____

_____

_____

D. Have you participated with an angel in its assignment?

Discussion

Angels and Jesus

POINTS TO NOTE

1. The ministry of Jesus Christ was closely associated with angels. Angel Gabriel announced His conception to the Virgin Mary, angels announced His birth to the shepherds, angels ministered to Him after the forty-day fast and temptation in the wilderness, angels were present at His tomb, at His resurrection, and they were present at His ascension to Heaven. Angels were the first to preach the good news of His resurrection from the dead. Furthermore we are told He will return to earth with the shout of the archangel. Revelation 1:1 gives credence to the value of angelic ministry in the overall weaponry of Christ
2. Angels must not be worshiped or prayed to (see Col. 2:18; Rev. 19:10, 22:9-9).
3. Angels will be taught by the church (see Eph. 3:10; 1 Cor. 4:9; 1 Pet. 1:10-12).

EXERCISES

A. How important a role did angels play in the life of Jesus Christ?

Discussion

B. Do you find the statement that angels will be taught by the church to contradict an earlier discussion regarding humans not being able to dictate to angels?

Discussion

_____

_____

_____

∽∾∽

∽ PRACTICAL PRINCIPLES AND DISCUSSION ∾

_____

_____

_____

_____

_____

_____

_____

_____

_____

_____

_____

_____

_____

CHAPTER 19

How to Engage Angels

 POINTS TO NOTE

1. The Bible gives clear rules on what angels are, what they do, how they do what they do, how we are to relate to them, and at whose commands they are moved. In the present dispensation, angels revolve around the establishment of the Church of Jesus Christ and in advancing and building up the Body of Christ (see Exod. 23:20-21).

2. Angels heed the voice of the Word of God. We should know that angels are not sentimental—they are heavenly assistants sent forth under strict instruction to carry out assignments. They could be on assignment independent of human action, but most times they are on conditional assignments, the eventual outcome of which depends on human actions or reactions. God respects the human right of choice. Jesus said, *"Or do you think that I cannot now pray to My Father, and He will provide Me with more than twelve legions of angels?"* (Matt. 26:53 NKJV).

3. We do not command the release of angels, we pray to God to release angels. When we pray and ask God for help, He dispatches angels to deliver us from the enemy. As we see in Psalm 35:5, *"Let them be as chaff before the wind, and let the angel of the Lord chase them."* A tremendous New Testament example of this is found in the story of the apostle Peter who was delivered from prison by an angel (see Acts 12).

 EXERCISES

A. What are angels? What do they do? How do they do what they do? How are you supposed to relate to them? At whose commands they are released?

Discussion

_____

_____

_____

B. Angels can be on an assignment independent of human action; but most times they are on conditional assignments—the outcome depending on human actions or reactions. Is this because God respects humans' right of choice?

Discussion

_____

_____

_____

C. Do not command the release of angels; rather, pray to God to release angels. When you pray and ask God for help, He dispatches angels to deliver you from the enemy.

Discussion

_____

_____

_____

⤫

Relating to Angels

 POINTS TO NOTE

1. When relating to angels, remember:

> - Ask God to release them through prayers.
> - Use the Word of God because angels harken to the voice of God's Word.
> - Angels work in the name of the Lord.
> - Angels can give us guidance from God.
> - Angels can bring promises of God to us on earth.
> - We do not worship angels nor build memorials for them.
> - We should speak the will of God when relating to angels.
> - We should speak the word of faith when relating to angels.
> - Maintain a right standing with God.
> - Be sensitive in the spirit to know the now will of God on the issue.
> - That angels are not only encamping around us, they are also listening to what we say.

2. Angels are indirectly empowered by the prayers of the saints (see Dan. 10:7-14; Acts 12:5-11). The Church prayed to God and the angel was released. Daniel prayed and humbled himself, it was heard in Heaven and an angel was released (see Rev. 8:3-4 NKJV).

3. Disobedience provokes angels (see Gen. 19:15-17; Luke 17:29-32). Angels are provoked when the Word of God or His promises are not mixed with faith, (see Exod. 23:20-21), and when we resist them in their assignment from God (see Luke 1:11-15). Angels are also provoked when negative words or words contrary to the Word or will of God are spoken (see Eccl. 5:1-2 and 5:6). Doubts or unbelief will bind your angels.

 EXERCISES

A. Has the bulleted list given you a better perspective about angels and their functions and your relationship with them?

Discussion

_____

_____

_____

B. Do you have a better understanding about how important your prayers to God are in relating with angels?

Discussion

_____

_____

_____

C. What steps will you take—today and every day—not to provoke the angels?

Discussion

_____

_____

_____

∽ PRACTICAL PRINCIPLES AND DISCUSSION ∽

CHAPTER 20

Handling Revelations In Local Congregation

 POINTS TO NOTE

1. All revelations, including visual ones relating to the local congregation, should be recorded and evaluated by the leadership. Interpretations should be sought and judged. Once the interpretation has been accepted as true, it should be recorded alongside other revelations and only acted upon when it has been confirmed, except when the interpretation itself is a confirmation of a previous revelation. Confirmation is a further revelation on a subject either by prophecy, another dream/vision, or current events. Periodic review of visual revelations and their interpretation should be conducted.

2. The timing and implementation of any prophecy, including picture revelations relating to the local congregation, rests on the apostolic and pastoral anointing of the leadership. There are several reasons why this should be:

   - Every warning revelation, whether in dreams/visions or other forms of revelations, comes with some degree of divinely inbuilt urgency to the recipient that requires apostolic or pastoral moderation.

   - The apostles and pastors usually have access to other prophetic revelations that the individual watchman or prophet may not be aware of. Therefore, the apostles and pastors who oversee many prophets see many parts of the whole but the individual prophet sees only his part.

 EXERCISES

A. What type of visual revelations have you experienced? Have you sought interpretation?

Discussion

_____

_____

_____

B. What role does your pastoral leadership play in the interpretation of revelations from God?

Discussion

_____

_____

_____

Avoiding Individual and Corporate Errors of Judgment

POINTS TO NOTE

1. It is best to handle revelations while under pastoral covering. Abundance of revelation most often leads to spiritual pride if a person is not seasoned in the gifting: *"To keep me from becoming conceited because of these surpassingly great revelations, there was given me a thorn in my flesh, a messenger of Satan, to torment me"* (2 Cor. 12:7). It is spiritual pride to think that the little part God reveals to us is the whole story. Some young prophets have shipwrecked their careers by becoming prideful and not submitting to their pastor.

2. Visual revelations, especially dreams and visions, have played major roles in the deliverance and the prophetic guidance of many nations (see Judg. 7:9-16; Gen. 12:1-6). On a corporate level, we need to understand that revelations are divinely given for God's purposes and that they can come through dreams, visions, trances, impressions, a flash of ideas, word of God, and in many other diverse ways. What is important is that we can ride on revelations that are received by other people, provided it is authenticated as truly God-given revelation (see 2 Peter 1:19-21).

EXERCISES

A. What examples came to your mind of spiritual pride when you read number 1? Could you be found guilty of self-conceitedness for neglecting revelatory guidance from God just because you did not personally receive the revelation, even though, for all intents and purposes, such revelations have been properly validated, both in source and content?

Discussion

_____

_____

_____

B. Are you serious about gaining proper understanding of all revelation so that you can avail yourself of God's intended benefits?

Discussion

_____

_____

_____

❧❧❧

PRACTICAL PRINCIPLES AND DISCUSSION

_____

_____

_____

_____

_____

_____

_____

_____

_____

_____

_____

_____

_____

_____

_____

CHAPTER 21

Avoiding Demonic Influences

 POINTS TO NOTE

1. The following are steps to take to avoid demonic influences and encourage angelic activity in your everyday life: 1) avoid demonic practices such as consulting magicians, enchanters, sorcerers, and astrologers; 2) avoid vile and unholy imagery such as pornography, lewd activities, and abusive situations; 3) be mindful what you listen to (see Dan. 3:8-20) as Jesus said in Luke 8:18; 4) avoid evil company because it corrupts; 5) do not associate with accursed things such as the case in Joshua 7:10-12.

2. Corrupted wisdom is menacing us every day at an alarming rate. The difficulty is that often the miracles of healings, financial breakthroughs, raising the dead, or other supernatural signs make a spectacle of the sovereignty and supremacy of God. That in itself is desirable, but it is also the avenue by which satan lures many into excesses and self-exaltation.

3. Sexual bondage creeps in subtly and overwhelms its victims with such a passion that reason and logic are easily thrown into the abyss. A sanctified imagination is important for receiving and handling revelations from God whereas a corrupted imagination, emanating from sexual sin, pollutes the imagination making a person's reception blurred and distorted so that prophets stumble at giving prophecy. Do not allow sexual sin or inordinate sexual indulgence to subvert your walk with God.

 EXERCISES

A. Of the five steps listed, which are the hardest for you to adapt? The easiest? Why?

Discussion

_____

_____

_____

B. The functionality of giftedness in a person attracts the attention and attacks from the enemy of your soul. What can you do to consistently win every battle?

Discussion

_____

_____

_____

C. Are you or do you know someone who is in sexual bondage? Do you think this particular demonic influence is more prevalent today than in past decades?

Discussion

_____

_____

_____

∽◦∽

∽ PRACTICAL PRINCIPLES AND DISCUSSION ∽

_____

_____

_____

_____

_____

_____

_____

_____

_____

_____

_____

CHAPTER 22

Handling Strange Events

 POINTS TO NOTE

1. There is an increasing occurrence of strange events in the last days—most of which are described in the Bible. The Living Bible translation puts this rather clearly: *"And I will cause strange demonstrations in the heavens and on the earth"* (Acts 2:19); *"and put strange symbols in the earth and sky"* (Joel 2:30). Strange events come in various forms and in varying degrees of strangeness or awesomeness. Most strange events serve to emphasize the sovereignty and supremacy of God, yet in many other instances, the strangeness or bizarre nature of the spiritual encounter seems not to be God's first choice. Some of God's messages may assume strange or bizarre forms, possibly to compel humankind to pay attention to what God might want to say.

2. A majority of strange events occur in the "twilight zone"—a state that is not clearly defined or demarcated between the spirit and the natural realms. Twilight zone visionary experiences are difficult to define, whether they occur in the spirit or in the natural realm. Most occur in-between the boundaries of the two realms. Twilight zone visionary events come in various forms, strangeness, or awesomeness, and often show differing degrees of involvement of the physical realm. This is why the apostle Paul was blind for three days following his Damascus road visionary encounter (also see 2 Cor. 12:1-5) and why patriarch Jacob limped the rest of his life after wrestling with the angel of the Lord.

3. The following are examples of biblical strange events:

    *   *Translation,* transporting from one place to another or to convey to Heaven without natural death (see Hebrews 11:5 KJV; 2 Kings 2:11-12; Ezekiel 8:1-7; Acts 8:39; 1 Kings 18:44-46; Acts 16:6-10).

    *   *Apparition,* a visionary encounter in which a supernatural happening becomes perceptible to the natural eyes. An apparition happens because the supernatural event has sufficiently involved and permeated the physical realm to the extent that it makes it possible to be seen by the natural eyes. An example is when an angel assumes a temporal appearance (see Daniel 3:20-25; 5:5-7).

    *   *Carry-over,* when an event or occurrence in the spiritual encounter is carried over into the physical realm (see Genesis 32:22-32; Daniel 7:28).

    *   *Dream-like state visionary encounter,* such as when Peter was miraculously released from jail and he walked out of the jail and passed through the iron gate before he came into his natural senses (see Acts 12:7-12 NKJV).

    *   *Transfiguration,* is when an earthly vessel transforms to take on a temporary heavenly appearance. Thus the Bible speaks of the heavenly appearance that once came upon Jesus, in His humanity, during His earthly ministry (see Matthew 17:2-9 NKJV, also see Acts 6:15).

EXERCISES

A. Have you personally experienced strange events, or have you been told of such? Do you think God was trying to get your—or someone else's—attention?

Discussion

_____

_____

_____

B. After reading Second Corinthians 12:1-5, how would you define Paul's experience? How do you define the third heaven he mentions?

Discussion

_____

_____

_____

C. Do you believe the biblical strange events listed are happening today? Why or why not?

Discussion

_____

_____

_____

∾ PRACTICAL PRINCIPLES AND DISCUSSION ∾

CHAPTER 23

Embracing God's Signs, Wonders, and Miracles

 POINTS TO NOTE

1. The Bible says God will show forth wonders in heavens and signs on earth. However, signs and wonders are not seals of divinity. Important considerations:

> • A *miracle* is an event that appears unexplained by the laws of nature and so is held to be supernatural in origin or an act of God.
>
> • A *wonder* is defined as that which arouses awe, astonishment, or admiration, or something strange.
>
> • A *sign* is a pointer, like a signpost, confirming the Word of God and directs man's attention to Christ.

Whether a divine sign, a wonder, or a miracle, they all transcend the limits of natural logic and may serve to confirm the supernaturalness, supremacy, and sovereignty of God (see Dan. 4:3a; Exod. 4:8 KJV). A sign from God has "voice," and clearly God's objective in giving the sign is to speak to us. Though signs are supernatural signals from Heaven, they happen in the natural and are therefore easily missed.

2. The first and most important factor that influences whether a person is able or not to recognize a divinely orchestrated strange event, is the state of person's heart. Those whose hearts are not yielded to the truth of Christ are less likely to distinguish divine from satanic strange events (see 2 Thess. 2:10-11).

   • Divine strange events reveal the glory of God (see John 2:11), but magic miracles and wonders do not, they draw people away from God.

   • Divine strange events draw attention to something God is doing that otherwise might have been missed.

   • Divine strange events increase our faith in God and draw us closer to Him as exemplified by what happened to the disciples (see John 2:22).

   • These divine events establish the authority or the sovereignty of God as illustrated by the demand of the Jews (see John 2:18). On the one hand, magic miracles create fear and binds people to the bonds of the gods and their evil covenants.

   • Divine strange events bring people to the knowledge of God (see Rom. 15:18-19).

- They draw people to the majesty of God.

- They exalt the name of God.

- They bring reverence to God.

- They bring reassurance of the character of God: love, kindness, compassion, mercy, and forgiveness.

- Divine strange events are often a one-time occurrence, divinely made for the particular situation.

- The focus is never on the human being even though the divine strange happening may be distinctively associated with the person; for example, the healing power of God in the crusade of an evangelist associated with healing anointing may manifest even before the evangelist arrives at the crusade arena.

3. Beware! Signs, wonders, and miracles are not always of God. As the Bible says, *"This man of sin will come as Satan's tool, full of satanic power and will trick everyone with **strange demonstrations** and will do great miracles"* (2 Thess. 2:9 LB). Always be alert and have a discerning spirit as satan's ability to pretend is probably far beyond human comprehension: *"And no wonder, for Satan himself masquerades as an angel of light"* (2 Cor. 11:14). Also the Bible admonishes us to *"Be of sober spirit, be on the alert. Your adversary, the devil, prowls around like a roaring lion, seeking someone to devour"* (1 Peter 5:8 NASB; also see Acts 19:11-20; 1 Samuel 28:5-19).

 EXERCISES

A. Based on what you have read in this manual and in the Bible, write your own definitions of signs, wonders, and miracles.

Discussion

_____

_____

_____

B. How would you describe the "state of your heart"? What improvements, if any, could you make?

Discussion

_____

_____

_____

C. How good are you at discerning the spirit of satan from the Spirit of God regarding signs, wonders, and miracles? What steps can you take to increase your discernment?

Discussion

_____

_____

_____

❦

❧ PRACTICAL PRINCIPLES AND DISCUSSION ❧

_____

_____

_____

_____

_____

_____

_____

_____

_____

_____

_____

_____

_____

_____

_____

PART III

How to Correct Injustice in Everyday Living

HOW YOU CAN LIVE AN EVERYDAY SUPERNATURAL LIFE

Introduction

In this fallen world we experience disharmony, a far cry from the original plan and purpose of God for humankind. Inharmonious circumstances of this world grimace at us as a bomb goes off in the Middle East, crumpled bodies lay motionless, and crying children wonder aimlessly on the street unsure of what the next moment holds. In Africa, pathetic scenes of starving families and mothers watching helplessly as precious children die from lack of food is a common sight. In the United States of America, ghetto violence continues and is assuming an epic dimension; and in Central America, the ages-long drug war is rapidly expanding and causing devastation in the lives of people bringing social disorder into a new high.

Many wrestle with the deepest of emotions as they ponder the perplexing question: *Where is God?* Indeed the prophet Malachi once pondered this same question (see Malachi 2:17). God has not finished with this planet, and we must hold steadfastly and wait on Him! In fact, the Bible infers that God places high premium on His ability to restore planet Earth to its original state of perfection! It is only when that time comes that we can say that history has truly ran its course. This is my conclusion: though the wicked may seem to succeed, their success won't last—in the long run, godliness will prevail.

Tough times may come, but *"the Lord is still in His holy temple and He rules from heaven. He watches everything that happens here on earth"* (Ps. 11:4 TLB). The Psalmist declares, *"Awake, my God; decree justice"* (Ps. 7:6b). Somehow, deep within every human being, whether Jew or Gentile, slave or free, old or young, black or white, male or female, is the anchor on which hangs our hope that someday justice will be done.

The notion that sooner or later every injustice will have a moment in the court of God is often the basis of our strength to face life each and every day. More often than not, when circumstances goes against us, we are quick to think that God is also against us, but we should remember this—humankind is limited, only God is transcendent. No matter what happens, God will always remain the God of justice. There is one undeniable fact—those who work according to God's precepts and commandments will not be disappointed!

We should also be comforted that God's justice is always tempered by His mercy. The prophet Jeremiah had a glimpse of this aspect of the justice of God when he prophesied hope beyond judgment to the Israelites: *"I am with you and will save you," declares the Lord. "Though I completely destroy all the nations among which I scatter you, I will not completely destroy you. I will discipline you but only with justice; I will not let you go entirely unpunished"* (Jer. 30:11). The prophet Isaiah spoke of the grace, mercy, and compassion that surrounds the justice of God when he said, *"Yet the Lord longs to be gracious to you; He rises to show you compassion. For the Lord is a God of justice. Blessed are all who wait for Him!"* (Isa. 30:18).

God allows us to brag on this, that we know Him as the God of justice. *"Let not the wise man boast of his wisdom or the strong man boast of his strength or the rich man boast of his riches, but let him who boasts boast about this: that he understands and knows Me, that I am the Lord, who exercises kindness, justice and righteousness on earth, for in these I delight," declares the Lord"* (Jer. 9:23-24).

This section of the manual is premised on the fact that God is capable of restoring supernatural order and harmony to every aspect of our lives from the failures consequent to Adam's disobedience at the Garden of Eden!

CHAPTER 24

Laying a Supernatural Foundation

 POINTS TO NOTE

1. Even in the present fallen world there are still undeniable echoes from the unspoiled world God had designed. These are reminders of the way things could have been. The original creation order and the splendor that Adam and Eve once enjoyed existed because God created the universe and placed all things in divine order and harmony (see Heb. 1:2 AMP).

2. To keep the harmony of the partnership between the earth and the heavens, God set rules to govern human-kind's behavior on earth. He came down in the cool of the evening to fellowship with man and woman as long as His rules were obeyed. If so, then they correctly related to God and to the heavens. The legitimate way of interacting with heavens from the earth is through the rules of God who holds the heavens and the earth together. Any other way is counterfeit.

 EXERCISES

A. Because God's justice is shrouded in mercy, compassion, and grace, how could the evil one so easily entice Eve to disobey God's instruction?

Discussion

_____

_____

_____

B. What are some undeniable echoes from God's unspoiled world that immediately come to mind?

Discussion

_____

_____

_____

C. The legitimate way of interacting with heavens from the earth is through the rules of God who holds the heavens and the earth together. How agreeable are you to abiding by His rules?

Discussion

_____

_____

_____

∽∼∾

∽ PRACTICAL PRINCIPLES AND DISCUSSION ∾

_____

_____

_____

_____

_____

_____

_____

_____

_____

_____

_____

_____

_____

_____

_____

CHAPTER 25

Heavenly Realms

First, Second, and Third Heavens

 POINTS TO NOTE

1. The first heaven is the physical heaven, consisting of the earth, the atmosphere of the earth and the sky. The earth is part of the terrestrial expanse we refer to as the first heaven (see Gen. 1:9,15). The earth is the domain of humanity's sphere of authority (see Ps. 115:16). The present earth shall pass away and a new earth shall be established.

2. The second heaven is the celestial expanse between the earth and the third heaven.

3. Geographically the second heaven refers the invisible expanse that covers the earth and lies beneath the third heaven. It does not belong to the devil; it was created by God and belongs to God (see Gen. 1:1; Col. 1:16; Ps. 114:16 NKJV), but it is the place from where the demonic forces exert their influences upon the earth (see Eph. 6:12). It is the zone of spiritual conflict.

4. The third heaven is the abode of God and the home of those who died in Christ. There are many parts of the third heaven mentioned in the Bible including the Throne Room (see Rev. 4:1-6; Isa. 6:1-4; Ezek. 1:19-28; 1 Kings 22:19-22; Zech. 3:7; Rev. 20:4), the holy mountains, the Mount of Congregation, and the cloud of heaven that includes cities, rivers, streets, and mansions (see Ezek. 28:14; Isa. 14:13).

5. God is committed to reclaiming this fallen world and rescuing sinful people through His son Jesus Christ and promises a new earth and a new heaven (see Isa. 65:17). We are to repent and turn toward God (see Acts 3:19-21) and take each day seriously (see 2 Pet. 3:10-14). By word of knowledge revelation John and the prophet Isaiah describe harmony in Christians' future home (see Rev. 21:1-2; Isa. 11:6-9).

EXERCISES

A. The earth is the expanse in which dew and frost form, the birds fly, and the winds blow, but it extends to the regions of outer space where stellar bodies, the sun, the moon, and the stars are,¹ as mentioned in Deuteronomy 4:19: *"And when you look up to the sky and see the sun, the moon and the stars—all the heavenly array—...."* Are you familiar with the term first heaven?

Discussion

_____

_____

_____

B. *"For our struggle is not against flesh and blood, but against the rulers, against the authorities, against the powers of this dark world and against the spiritual forces of evil in the heavenly realms."* How familiar are you with the term second heaven?

Discussion

_____

_____

_____

C. *"Then I saw a new heaven and a new earth, for the first heaven and the first earth had passed away, and there was no longer any sea. I saw the Holy City, the New Jerusalem, coming down out of heaven from God, prepared as a bride beautifully dressed for her husband."* Like John and after prayerful consideration, describe the new heaven and new earth in your own words.

Discussion

_____

_____

_____

PRACTICAL PRINCIPLES AND DISCUSSION

CHAPTER 26

Connecting Heavens and Earth

 POINTS TO NOTE

1. We live on earth, and God's throne is in the highest heaven, the third heaven! To interact, we have to break through the covering interface between the earth and God's throne. This zone of spiritual warfare is the second heaven—a spiritual trading place for blessings and evil (see Eph. 6:12).

2. Though invisible, the heavenly places are as real as the visible and tangible earth in which we live. There is constant interaction between the earth and the heavens that can either be enhanced or clouded by spiritual forces. Also, things we do in the natural world can either hinder the connection or enhance its communications (see Deut. 28:23 NKJV; Gen. 28:10-17).

3. By availing ourselves to an open heaven (see Gen. 28:10-17), we can experience the clarity of revelations in a place reflecting the openness of the third heaven, as did Jacob. An open heaven can also mean other material and immaterial blessings from the third heaven. An opening of the heavens is the bypassing of the hindrances of the second heaven to connect God's abode with the earth.

 EXERCISES

A. Do you think there were three heavens before the Fall in the Garden of Eden?

Discussion

_____

_____

_____

B. Do you believe that the things you do in the natural world can either hinder the connection or enhance communications in the spiritual realm?

Discussion

_____

_____

_____

C. How familiar are you with the term open heaven? Describe it in your own words after reading Genesis 28:10-17.

Discussion

_____

_____

_____

⤳⤳⤳

Heavenly Places

 POINTS TO NOTE

1. *Heavenly places* is a descriptive term that refers to the invisible realm of the heavens and technically would include the second and the third heaven and other invisible realms of hell (see Eph. 6:23, 3:10, 2:6, 1:20).

2. Things that may exist in or transit through the heavenly places include:

   • The dews of heavens (see Zech. 8:12).

   • Spiritual blessings (see Eph. 1:3).

   • Principalities, powers and wickedness (see Eph. 6:12).

   • Divine revelations in transit (see Dan. 9:20-23).

   • Prophets on divinely inspired spiritual encounters (see Ezek. 8:1-3).

   • Other people (see Acts 16:6-10).

   • Warring angels (see Num. 22:21-22).

   • The angel with drawn sword (see Josh. 5:13-14; 1 Chron. 21:16).

   • Waters (see Gen. 1:7).

   • Curses (see Prov. 26:2).

   The third heaven can be open over a place on a permanent basis when it is called a *heavenly portal* or can be open over a place on a temporary basis.

3. Ultimately, the Lord Jesus will return and all evil will be banished; then heavenly places will be filled with the glory of God (see Eph. 3:10).

EXERCISES

A. This definition of heavenly realms includes invisible realms of hell—do you agree with this definition? Why or why not?

Discussion

_____

_____

_____

B. Regarding the previous question, do some of the Scripture passages in number 2 prove or disprove your answer?

Discussion

_____

_____

_____

C. What mental image comes to your mind when you read the words "Lord Jesus will return and all the heavens will be filled with His glory"?

Discussion

_____

_____

_____

∽∾∽

∾ PRACTICAL PRINCIPLES AND DISCUSSION ∾

_____

_____

_____

_____

_____

CHAPTER 27

Approaching and Accessing Heavenly Realms

 ## POINTS TO NOTE

1. There is divine partnership between the earth and the heavens, and God Himself regulates this partnership. The only way to truly participate in this partnership *legally* is to get permission from God. Illegal participation is possible but it is of the devil and is demonic—this is why we need to continuously sanctify and consecrate ourselves to gain legal access into the heavenly realm.

2. *Spiritual sanitation* is the removal of all things that are against the expression of the pure spirituality of God in our lives. We are spiritual beings having a natural experience, so our true nature should be to break the hold of our sinfulness and allow the expression of divine attributes of God in our everyday lives.

3. God can abolish every human act that is contrary to His intention for our lives. God has rules and a strict code of standards of wrongs and rights that no one can escape, and if we work them rightly, they will work for us. It does not matter how or when we start, it is how we finish that counts. No matter what may come your way, our God works for good for those who love Him.

 ## EXERCISES

A. What is the difference between a legal and an illegal partnership relationship with the earth and heavens?

Discussion

_____

_____

_____

B. Spiritual sanctification is breaking the hold of sinfulness and allowing the expression of divine attributes of God in our everyday lives. How sanctified do you feel today?

Discussion

_____

_____

_____

C. Because God can abolish every human act that is contrary to His intention for your life, do you allow Him access into every aspect of your mind, body, and soul?

Discussion

_____

_____

_____

⌘

Approach with Spoken Words

POINTS TO NOTE

1. A very direct way of approaching the heavenly realm is by spoken words. Words can ascend as spiritual arrows into the heavenly places, and we can approach or appeal to God to bring justice to any injustice in our lives or plead with God for mercy, which is His exception from judgment (see Dan. 2:18).

2. The words of a righteous person avail much and are capable of ascending unto the heaven. Jesus says the words He speaks are spirits and that they have life (see John 6:63). Those with clean hands and who harbor no iniquity in their hearts, God will hear when they pray—their words are capable of ascending unto the holy hills of God. As we cannot ascend with our earthen bodies, we ascend in the spirit commonly by sending words to the heavenlies.

3. pure heart clears the way for our word to ascend to the heavenlies and reach God. The purity of your heart determines your relationship with the Father in heaven and the ability to contend with the spiritual forces of evil in heavenly realm (see Dan. 10:11).

EXERCISES

A. Speaking is a very direct why to approach the heavenly realm. How often do you use this pathway to God?

Discussion

_____

_____

_____

B. How clean are your hands? Are you harboring any iniquity in your heart?

Discussion

_____

_____

_____

C. The purity of your heart determines your relationship with the Father in heaven and the ability to defeat the spiritual forces of evil in heavenly realm. How pure is your heart?

Discussion

_____

_____

_____

∽∾∿

Walking in Humility

 POINTS TO NOTE

1. There are four basic requirements to approach the heavenlies mentioned in Second Chronicles 7:13-15 as necessary for God to hear our petition in heaven: humility, prayers, seeking the face of God, and turning away from evil. With these requirements in place, God will respond by: hearing in heaven, forgiving our sins, healing the land, and turning His eyes and ears toward us.

2. Other ways to access the heavenly realms include inputting and influencing the happenings in the heavenly realm via the prophetic privilege of intercession. Prophetic privilege of intercession is the art of using the privilege of a revelation as the platform for interceding for what is revealed. However, this by implication involves operating in prophetic anointing, or in the spirit of prophecy (the testimony of Jesus) (see Acts 10:2-4).

EXERCISES

A. Of the four requirements—humility, prayers, seeking the face of God, and turning away from evil—which one is the hardest for you to adhere to?

Discussion

_____

_____

_____

B. Prophetic privilege of intercession is the art of using the privilege of a revelation as the platform for interceding for what is revealed. Have you been gifted with this privilege?

Discussion

_____

_____

_____

ᘓᘔᘓ

PRACTICAL PRINCIPLES AND DISCUSSION

_____

_____

_____

_____

_____

_____

_____

_____

_____

CHAPTER 28

The Power of the Spoken Word

 POINTS TO NOTE

1. Spoken words come in various levels of strength and in different ways and are like spiritual arrows into the unseen world that can bring good or harmful consequences upon humankind in the natural world. The words you speak can rescue you in times of trouble (see Prov. 12:6).

2. We sow seeds of spoken words every time we speak—words control the world. That being true, often the enemy will try to shoot wrong and negative thoughts into our minds so as to get us to speak them. Then he sits back to watch as we reap what we say. What we say can trigger things in the hands of the devil and his system—or in the hands of the Almighty God and His Kingdom agents.

3. Even angels are activated to act on our behalf by the words of our mouth: *"angels... harken to the voice of His word"* (Ps. 103:20). Spoken words are the means by which we give voice to the word of God on earth, and angels are great instruments of justice in the hands of God—what we say or don't say can hinder or activate angels meant to minister to us.

 EXERCISES

A. Do your words more often get you into trouble—or rescue you from trouble?

Discussion

_____

_____

_____

B. Do your words most often bring delight to the evil one—or the Almighty God?

Discussion

_____

_____

_____

C. Because angels are great instruments of justice in the hands of God, what you say or don't say can hinder or activate angels meant to minister to you. Do you believe this?

Discussion

_____

_____

_____

༄ཅ

Spoken Words

POINTS TO NOTE

1. Spoken words are spirit—they are invisible and operate in a way you may not be able to see, but they can have lasting effects. Spirits don't die. Also, spoken words have life. They are made of spiritual substance and can perpetuate and maintain themselves either in dormant or active forms.

2. A dormant spoken word exists only in the spirit realm waiting for the right condition to manifest in the natural realm or to be fulfilled in the natural realm. It is our responsibility to activate the dormant words of blessings over our lives. One ways to do this is to ensure we comply with the divine requirement for it to be fulfilled—then speak it into being.

3. It is by spoken words that blessings or inheritance are conferred on a person or on a generation. God spoke blessing on Abraham and Abraham spoke the blessing on Isaac. Isaac blessed Jacob by the power of the spoken word. Jacob also blessed his children with spoken words. Our words can bring immediate response from the throne of God, as the angel told the prophet Daniel that his words triggered response in heaven on the very day he spoke them (see Dan. 10:12).

EXERCISES

A. Spoken words are spirit and they have life. How spirit-filled and live-giving are your daily words and normal conversations?

Discussion

_____

_____

_____

B. Are you in the habit of activating the dormant words of blessings over your life?

Discussion

_____

_____

_____

C. Is it possible that your lack of spoken words are hindering blessings or inheritance for you or your generation?

Discussion

_____

_____

_____

⤞⤝

God's Spoken Words

 POINTS TO NOTE

1. Many Scriptures refer to God's spoken words and how vital they were for all those who heard and believed. See Isaiah 55:10-11; Hebrews 4:12 AMP; Psalm 62:11; Jeremiah 23:29 Psalm 33:6; Proverbs 4:22; Psalm 29:3-9. This is why you imbed the qualities of God in every spiritual encounter you have with Him.

2. The deadly words of the evil one are also spirits, see Revelation 16:13-14. This is why the mere words from the wife of King Ahab, Jezebel, were sufficient to drive a powerful prophet like Elijah into a state of depression and almost to a point of suicide.

3. The effective power behind spoken words depends on several things:

    *   The speaker's right standing with God.

    *   The faith with which it is said. Note that the power of the spoken word of the devil is often related to how much fear it generates in a person.

    *   The state of the mouth of the speaker; perverse lips produce death, and righteous lips produce life.

    *   Was the word said inspired by God and is it birthed in the Holy Spirit? When the heart overflows the mouth speaks.

    *   Is what was said in line with the plans of God? No wisdom, no plans could work against that of God.

- The speaker's authority over the situation. Most of the power of the devil is derived on this premise: any sin in our lives that gives the devil a landing pad in our situation makes the power of the devil more effective.

The battle of spoken words can be easily seen when compared side by side:

GODLY WAY	EVIL WAY
By *spoken words* the heavens and the earth were created. Genesis 1	By *spoken words* satan deceived Eve to disobey God. Man and creation fell. Genesis 3
To redeem man and the fallen creation, *the Word* became flesh and dwelt among us. John 1:14	Satan could not counterfeit this. Satan is not a creator.
Jesus Christ said that *the words He spoke* are spirit and are life. John 6:63	*Satan's words* are also spirit but bring only death. Proverbs 12:6 Revelation 16:13-14
The tongue of man has the power of life and death. Proverbs 18:21	Satan can make a man say things that are detrimental to himself. Proverbs 18:21
Let the redeemed of the Lord *say so.*	Do not yield yourself as *a mouth piece for the devil,* like Job's wife.
The true prophet of God declares by the *spoken word.* 1 Kings 17:1	The false prophet, Jezebel, declares by *spoken words.* 1 Kings 19:1
The final victory of the mouth and word. Revelation 19:15-16	

EXERCISES

A. *"I put my word in your mouth." "I have put my words in your mouth and covered you with the shadow of my hand—I who set the heavens in place, who laid the foundations of the earth, and who say to Zion, 'You are my people'"* (Isaiah 51:16). Your calling and ministry are intimately connected with the power of the words that come from your mouth.

Discussion

_____

_____

_____

B. Allow no room for the evil one to assess your mind, thoughts, or words. Do you believe he is a very formidable foe?

Discussion

_____

_____

_____

C. When the heart overflows the mouth speaks—what is your heart overflowing with today?

Discussion

_____

_____

_____

∾ PRACTICAL PRINCIPLES AND DISCUSSION ∾

CHAPTER 29

Proclamations, Decrees, and Edicts

 POINTS TO NOTE

1. To bring divine justice to the earth, God institutes decrees, pronouncements, and commandments to regulate human behavior to ensure the strict standards of wrongs and rights and a code of conduct that applies to everyone. On the other hand, the devil and his agents also have decrees or pronouncements targeted to push people out of God's plan and bring chaos and confusion (see Prov. 12:6 NLT).

2. To verbalize an idea, word, or concept is called *declaration*, whether done privately or publicly, it has the power to activate a dormant promise or curse into kinetic motion of fulfillment. Declaration is the easiest and often the first step toward fulfilment of a promise. Declaration from the righteous can often be sufficient to counter the evil intentions of the the evil one.

3. A public declaration is a *proclamation*. A proclamation requires public witnessing and has a superior power than a declaration. Usually the public proclamation has both spiritual invisible and natural visible witnesses. Because of this, it can be quite powerful and much more difficult to counter if emanating from the evil one.

4. A *decree* is an authoritative order that has the force of law behind it and can come as a: ruling, announcement, declaration, verdict, judgment, order, or pronouncement. Decrees have varying levels of authority and power behind them. Anybody can issue a decree provided he or she has some authority to back it up. For instance, the head of the home can issue decrees for the household.

5. An *edict* is a decree that has a recognizable source of official backing. Consequently, edicts from an evil spiritual authority are harder to resist or nullify than ordinary decrees because they are associated with the evil power of the official backing that would need to be dealt with (see Dan. 6:6-7).

 EXERCISES

A. Why does God institute decrees, pronouncements, and commandments that apply to everyone on earth?

Discussion

_____

_____

_____

B. What is the difference between a proclamation and a declaration?

Discussion

_____

_____

_____

C. As a parent, can you issue a decree in your home? How about an edict for your community?

Discussion

_____

_____

_____

❧❧❧

Individual Proclamation Power

 POINTS TO NOTE

1. Not all spoken words have the same power; some words carry more power than others. Some spoken words are in fact almost empty, that is they carry no significant power. Empty proclamations are words spoken that are *not in consonance with the divine order of things*.

2. If we proclaim the wrong things, God and His angels can become angry with us: *"Suffer not thy mouth to cause the flesh to sin; neither say thou before the angel, that it was an error: wherefore should God be angry at thy voice and destroy the work of thine hands?"* (Eccl. 5:6 KJV).

3. *God's role* in the effectiveness of spoken words is paramount. God can annul or frustrate some spoken words if they come without the love of God and if they are pronounced against the purposes of God (see Exod. 4:12 KJV; Isa. 44:25-26; 1 Sam. 3:19).

4. Other factors that determine the power behind the spoken word include the following:

> - *The spiritual standing* of the person. That is right standing with God, the words of a righteous people carry weight.
> - *Faith with which the spoken word* was released. As the Bible says, *"'I believed; therefore I have spoken.' With that same spirit of faith we also believe and therefore speak"* (2 Cor. 4:13).
> - *The legal right of the person* over the matter.
> - Allowing the word to *be birthed in the presence of the Holy Spirit* before proclaiming it.

> • *Communion with the Holy Spirit.* Words are more powerful if confirmed by the Holy Spirit.
>
> • *Studying the word* helps to align spoken words with God's Word.
>
> • *Sanctioned in the heavenly.* It is important to wait for the word to be sanctioned in Heaven before releasing it.

 EXERCISES

A. Have there been times when you proclaimed and you felt the words were powerful and would make a difference in the Kingdom? Times when your words fell flat?

Discussion

_____

_____

_____

B. Have God and His angels ever been angry with you for proclaiming the wrong thing?

Discussion

_____

_____

_____

C. After studying the factors mentioned, which one(s) pricked you heart? Why?

Discussion

_____

_____

_____

Decrees

 POINTS TO NOTE

1. *Reversible decrees* are those that can be altered by human action, usually by appealing to God (see Dan. 4:24-27). *Irreversible decrees* are those that cannot be altered by any human action, as in the Ten Commandments (see Exod. 20:1-17; see also Luke 1:29-33; 1 Thess. 4:16-18). *Powerful decrees* are those that carry heavy spiritual consequences (see Dan. 4:13-17).

2. You can refuse to agree with the evil decrees so they cannot alight on you. In the story of Job, he immediately rebuked his wife in order to nullify her statement inspired by the devil (see Job 2:9-10; see also 1 Kings 22:13-14). These prophets did not allow the evil decrees to alight on them—they refused to cooperate with the evil decrees.

3. Another way to counter evil decrees is to issue a favorable decree or pronouncement in the same area that the evil decree addresses, as in the story of Esther (see Esther 8:9,11).

 EXERCISES

A. Can you think of additional biblical examples of reversible, irreversible, and powerful decrees?

Discussion

_____

_____

_____

B. Do you always refuse to agree or cooperate with evil decrees that someone says to you?

Discussion

_____

_____

_____

C. After you refuse to agree or cooperate with the evil decree, do you follow up with a favorable decree too nullify the evil one?

Discussion

_____

_____

_____

∾ PRACTICAL PRINCIPLES AND DISCUSSION ∾

CHAPTER 30

Passing the Torch

 POINTS TO NOTE

1. *Passing the torch* is a commonly used phrase when the head of a corporation passes on to his or her successor the staff of the leadership publicly among pomp and pageantry. In the physical realm this process is not haphazard; it follows a defined pattern. In the spirit realm passing the touch also follows biblical principles. Many ministries have suffered temporary shipwreck or even permanent shipwreck when there is a wrong exchange. Many may find it hard to comprehend, but there are strict spiritual principles guiding this process.

2. There are two types of DNA systems for the transference of inheritance in the ministry: the family DNA system and the spiritual DNA system. Psalm 139:13-16 mentions the knitting together in the mother's womb referring to what I call bloodline DNA. This system follows blood-related or biological principles. Whereas the spiritual DNA system follows spiritual principles, when the two systems are properly blended together and used under God's guidance, they do not conflict.

3. Jeremiah 1:4-5 is a reflection of spiritual DNA, which God spoke into humankind; it exists at individual level in every person. The term *formed* in the womb refers to bloodline DNA. The spiritual DNA system precedes the bloodline DNA system, that is, before the forming of the body. The Lord *knew and ordained* Jeremiah— and you—before the body was formed.

 EXERCISES

A. Have you been a recipient of a "torch"? Have you been the giver of a "torch"?

Discussion

_____

_____

_____

B. How do the two DNA systems work together to fulfill God's plan for humanity?

Discussion

_____

_____

_____

C. "*He has made everything beautiful in its time. He has also set eternity in the hearts of men, yet they cannot fathom what God has done from the beginning to end*" (Eccl. 3:11). How does this passage relate to the DNA discussion?

Discussion

_____

_____

_____

✿

Activating Your Spiritual DNA System

 POINTS TO NOTE

1. We must continuously keep our spiritual DNA in tune with the plans of God. Our interaction with the world system is via the expression of our bloodline DNA system, but God always speaks to our potentials inherent in our spiritual DNA to lead us to our destiny. As we pass through life, the bloodline DNA system may want to overshadow or even try to deny our spiritual DNA.

2. Apostle Paul must have wrestled with this tendency when he wrote, "*For what I do is not the good I want to do; no, the evil I do not want to do—this I keep on doing. Now if I do what I do not want to do, it is no longer I who do it, but it is sin living in me that does it. So I find this law at work: When I want to do good, evil is right there with me. For in my inner being I delight in God's law; but I see another law at work in the members of my body, waging war against the law of my mind and making me a prisoner of the law of sin at work within my members. What a wretched man I am! Who will rescue me from this body of death? Thanks be to God—through Jesus Christ our Lord! So then, I myself in my mind am a slave to God's law, but in the sinful nature a slave to the law of sin*" (Rom. 7:19-25).

3. King David overcame the evil consequences that emanated from the weakness inherent in his biological DNA system by reactivating his spiritual DNA system to bring himself in alignment with his divine destiny (see Ps. 51:7-12; 32:3-5).

	Exchange of the Staff of Authority Biblical Examples	
BATON EXCHANGE	**DNA SYSTEM INVOLVED**	**COMMENTS**
David / Solomon	Family with Spiritual DNA	Family DNA must be backed by spiritual DNA to be effective. **1 Chronicles 28:5**—*Of all my sons—and the Lord has given me many—he has chosen my son Solomon to sit on the throne of the kingdom of the Lord over Israel.*
David / Hezekiah	Spiritual DNA	Spiritual DNA can stand alone. **2 Kings 18:3-4**—*He did what was right in the eyes of the Lord,* **just as his father David had done.** *He removed the high places, smashed the sacred stones and cut down the Asherah poles. He broke into pieces the bronze snake Moses had made, for up to that time the Israelites had been burning incense to it. (It was called Nehushtan.)*
David / Jesus Christ	Spiritual DNA	**Mark 10:47**—*When he heard that it was Jesus of Nazareth, he began to shout, "Jesus, Son of David, have mercy on me!"*
Eli / his sons	Family DNA without spiritual DNA	Family DNA alone for the basis of transference of the staff of authority is insufficient. **1 Samuel 3:11-13**—*And the Lord said to Samuel: "See, I am about to do something in Israel that will make the ears of everyone who hears of it tingle. At that time I will carry out against Eli everything I spoke against his family—from beginning to end. For I told him that I would judge his family forever because of the sin he knew about; his sons made themselves contemptible, and he failed to restrain them.*
Eli / Samuel	Spiritual DNA without family DNA	Can stand alone. **1 Samuel 3:1**—*The boy Samuel ministered before the Lord under Eli. In those days the word of the Lord was rare; there were not many visions.* See also 1 Samuel 3:19-21.

Judah Iscariot / Matthias	None	Democratic decision. They did not wait as they were told to for the promised Holy Spirit. Matthias' election to replace Judas Iscariot as the twelfth disciple was the first and last time we heard about him. **Acts 1:21-26**—*Therefore it is necessary to choose one of the men who have been with us the whole time the Lord Jesus went in and out among us, beginning from John's baptism to the time when Jesus was taken up from us. For one of these must become a witness with us of his resurrection." So they proposed two men: Joseph called Barsabbas (also known as Justus) and Matthias. Then they prayed, "Lord, You know everyone's heart. Show us which of these two You have chosen to take over this apostolic ministry, which Judas left to go where he belongs." Then they cast lots, and the lot fell to Matthias; so he was added to the eleven apostles.*
Judas Iscariot / Saul of Tarsus	Spiritual DNA	Chosen by God as an apostle to the Gentiles. **Acts 26:15-18**—*"Then I asked, 'Who are you, Lord?' "'I am Jesus, whom you are persecuting,' the Lord replied. 'Now get up and stand on your feet. I have appeared to you to appoint you as a servant and as a witness of what you have seen of Me and what I will show you. I will rescue you from your own people and from the Gentiles. I am sending you to them to open their eyes and turn them from darkness to light, and from the power of Satan to God, so that they may receive forgiveness of sins and a place among those who are sanctified by faith in Me.'*
Elijah / Elisha	Spiritual DNA	Spiritual DNA can stand alone. **1 Kings 19:16**—*Also, anoint Jehu son of Nimshi king over Israel, and anoint Elisha son of Shaphat from Abel Meholah to succeed you as prophet.*

Elisha / Gehazi	None	The rod of Elisha did not flourish in the hands of Gehazi. Gehazi forfeited his inheritance.
		2 Kings 4:29-31—*Elisha said to Gehazi, "Tuck your cloak into your belt, take my staff in your hand and run. If you meet anyone, do not greet him, and if anyone greets you, do not answer. Lay my staff on the boy's face." But the child's mother said, "As surely as the Lord lives and as you live, I will not leave you." So he got up and followed her. Gehazi went on ahead and laid the staff on the boy's face, but there was no sound or response. So Gehazi went back to meet Elisha and told him, "The boy has not awakened."*
		2 Kings 5:26-27—*But Elisha said to him, "Was not my spirit with you when the man got down from his chariot to meet you? Is this the time to take money, or to accept clothes, olive groves, vineyards, flocks, herds, or menservants and maidservants? Naaman's leprosy will cling to you and to your descendants forever." Then Gehazi went from Elisha's presence and he was leprous, as white as snow.*
Moses / Joshua	Spiritual DNA	**Deuteronomy 31:1-3**—*Then Moses went out and spoke these words to all Israel: "I am now a hundred and twenty years old and I am no longer able to lead you. The Lord has said to me, 'You shall not cross the Jordan.' The Lord your God Himself will cross over ahead of you. He will destroy these nations before you, and you will take possession of their land. Joshua also will cross over ahead of you, as the Lord said.*

 EXERCISES

A. Do you continuously keep your spiritual DNA in tune with the plans of God? Your bloodline DNA system may want to overshadow or even try to deny your spiritual DNA.

Discussion

_____

_____

_____

B. *"Now if I do what I do not want to do, it is no longer I who do it, but it is sin living in me that does it. So I find this law at work: When I want to do good, evil is right there with me. For in my inner being I delight in God's law; but I see another law at work in the members of my body, waging war...."* At times, do you think or say the same as Apostle Paul?

Discussion

_____

_____

_____

C. Are you cognizant of the evil consequences that emanate from the weakness inherent in your biological DNA system? Do you proactively reactivate your spiritual DNA system to bring yourself in alignment with God's divine destiny for your life?

Discussion

_____

_____

_____

❧❧❧

❧ PRACTICAL PRINCIPLES AND DISCUSSION ❧

_____

_____

_____

_____

_____

_____

_____

_____

PART IV

THE CHANGING
STRUGGLES
CONFRONTING
HUMANITY

HOW YOU CAN LIVE AN EVERYDAY SUPERNATURAL LIFE

Introduction

In our effort to live supernatural, everyday lives, we must realize that the earth can either rise up against humanity, or it can be subdued by humankind in the service of God. The choice belongs to those who are redeemed by the blood of Jesus Christ to influence the course of history. The eventual history of the planet Earth is being written by our actions today, recorded and preserved for us like a picture album that tells the story of every generation, whether good or bad. The Book of Job says, *"The heavens will expose his guilt; the earth will rise up against him"* (Job 20:27). This is a key statement because it warns us that when the heavens expose our guilt, the earth is then empowered to rise against us. We must stay in the place of obedience to God, exercising our dominion and subduing the earth.

In a certain region of Alaska, the sun did not rise for an unprecedented length of time. The sunset lasted for 65 days, from November 2006 to January 2007. The people were devastated by the prolonged period of darkness. I believe these 65 days of darkness, though limited only to a small region of the earth, serve as a warning to humanity.

We may be reminded of the prophecy of Isaiah against Babylon and how the fierce anger of the Lord will cause the stars of Heaven and their constellations to withhold their light with a darkening of the sunrise. *"See, the day of the Lord is coming—a cruel day, with wrath, and fierce anger—to make the land desolate and destroy the sinners with it. The stars of heaven and their constellations will not show their light. The rising sun will be darkened and the moon will not give its light"* (Isa. 13:9-10). We can no longer sit back, do nothing, and assume that these things are accidents of geography or climate or time.

You may ask, *"Is the earth angry with its inhabitants?"* We cannot ignore the increasing evidence of real life experiences and the many scriptural examples of the cosmic confrontations between earth and man. Imagine for instance, what will happen if the very ground on which we stand turns against us? I believe our greatest threat lies not in man-made weapons because these can be counteracted by equally brilliant human devices. The real weapons of mass destruction lie in the domain outside the wisdom of man—in the blind spot of scientific technology. This is why it is said that the wisdom of this world will come to nothing when the unpredictable rising of nature comes against humanity.

The prophet Jeremiah once saw how destroyed the earth could become if men were to walk away from the ordinances of God, without repentance, and walk into the arms of the devil. He saw a sort of cosmic cataclysm and a return to the primeval chaos (reminiscent of Genesis chapter 1) and so he cried out, warning the people of Judah to repent and return to the Lord.

My people are fools; they do not know me. They are senseless children; they have no understanding. They are skilled in doing evil; they know not how to do good. I looked at the earth, and it was formless and empty; and at the heavens, and their light was gone. I looked at the mountains, and they were quaking; all the hills were swaying. I looked, and there were no people; every bird in the sky had flown away. I looked, and the fruitful land was a desert; all its towns lay in ruins before the Lord, before His fierce anger. This is what the Lord says: "The whole land will be ruined, though I will not destroy it completely. Therefore the earth will mourn and the heavens above grow dark, because I have spoken and will not relent, I have decided and will not turn back" (Jeremiah 4:22-28).

I feel like the prophet Jeremiah, calling humanity to be alert to the ploy of the enemy, to break the secret bubble, and reveal the shapes of warfare to come. Apostle John, on the island of Patmos, had a vision of the future and the inevitable cosmic involvement in future warfare. The Book of Revelation records that through angelic intervention, God could use the sun as an instrument of judgment. *"The fourth angel poured out his bowl on the sun, and the sun was given power to scorch people with fire"* (Rev. 16:8).

The Book of Revelation is the picture of the future Church of Christ, but most people have failed to see that a significant proportion of it is devoted to the cosmic dimension of the future war. *"Every island fled away and the mountains could not be found. From the sky huge hailstones of about a hundred pounds each fell upon men..."* (Rev. 16:20-21). We must not allow the things that are supposed to bless us to become instruments of judgment or punishment upon us.

The future warfare will be fought on multiple, shifting, and elusive frontiers in keeping with the nature of man's chief adversary—the devil. Apart from the emerging cosmic dimension of spiritual warfare, there are the unfolding mind games being waged by the devil on humankind and the increasing angelic involvement in the affairs of men on earth. These crucial subjects are discussed in this book.

The final showdown is prophesied and recorded in the Book of Revelation:

> *When the thousand years are over, Satan will be released from his prison and will go out to deceive the nations in the four corners of the earth—Gog and Magog—to gather them for battle. In number they are like the sand on the seashore. They marched across the breadth of earth and surrounded the camp of God's people, the city He loves. But fire came down from heaven and devoured them. And the devil, who deceived them, was thrown into the lake of burning sulphur where the beast and the false prophet had been thrown. They will be tormented day and night forever and ever* (Revelation 20:7-10).

The events preceding this constitute *the countdown*. However, no one knows the time the Father has set for this; but the period between now and when the events are played out, is what I have described as *the final frontiers*.

The book that this section of the manual is taken from is a peep into the future. It is a glimpse of the emerging cosmic involvement of the seemingly docile elements of nature in warfare and how they could completely alter the way we do warfare. In preparation for this warfare, we need to understand the dynamics of the believer's authority, the spiritual domain of influence, and the kingdom of darkness and its methods of operation. The power of proclamation and the elemental forces of nature, such as the ground, the sun, the ancient mountains, the moon, and the deep water beneath, are also divine weapons in God's arsenal to bless humankind, but sadly they could become instruments of His judgment!

This section of the manual provides you with a practical approach to the changing struggles that may confront humanity in our future.

CHAPTER 31

Origin of the War on Earth

 POINTS TO NOTE

1. Somewhere along the line in the cosmic existence before Adam was created, lucifer, the angel who later became known as the devil or satan, got the idea of taking the place of God. Because of his exceptional beauty and wisdom, he became corrupted and desired to usurp the throne of God. He led a third of the angels in Heaven in rebellion against God. Archangel Michael and the remaining angelic beings loyal to God fought and defeated lucifer. Together with his rebel angels, lucifer was cast out of Heaven (see Rev. 12:7-12).

2. It is possible that during the rebellion of satan the world became chaotic and distorted, and the seven days of creation in Genesis 1:1 may actually be an account of God restoring the earth to a habitable state after the war. But in Genesis 1:2, *"Now the earth was formless and empty, darkness was over the surface of the deep, and the Spirit of God was hovering over the waters."* The prophet Ezekiel spoke about satan while prophesying about the king of Tyre, who had become an agent of satan on earth (see Ezek. 28:12-18).

3. Many people believe the theory that millions of years exists between Genesis 1:1 and Genesis 1:2, and that the formlessness and emptiness mentioned in Genesis 1:2 was the result of the cosmic war between lucifer and his agents and Michael and the loyal angels. To the glory of God, even in that formless state, the Spirit of God hovered over the deep and held things in place.

 EXERCISES

A. Do you know people, who have been overcome by their own beauty and wisdom, who have rebelled against God? What was their fate?

Discussion

_____

_____

_____

B. Do you think that the seven days of creation in Genesis 1:1 may actually be an account of God restoring the earth to a habitable state after the war?

Discussion

_____

_____

_____

C. Are you one of the people who believe the theory that millions of years exists between Genesis 1:1 and Genesis 1:2? Why or why not?

Discussion

_____

_____

_____

⤳⤳⤳

The Great Deception and the Fall of Humankind

 POINTS TO NOTE

4. 1. After six days of creation, God emphatically saw that "it was good" (see Gen. 1:25). God had made man in His image and gave him dominion over the earth. True to satan's rebellious nature, he rejected this scenario, deceived Adam and Eve into disobeying God, and usurped humankind's dominion on earth.

5. 2. After the Fall, God cursed satan and turned this once-anointed cherub into a serpent (see Gen. 3:14). In addition, God put enmity between satan and humankind (see Gen. 3:15). The serpent is a dust eater and feeds on the flesh—because the human body came from the dust of the earth, we should make deliberate effort not to yield our body to the devil as instruments of wickedness, providing satan a free meal.

6. 3. Always look for the source whenever the challenges of life come across your path. The enemy will attack using those close to you, as well as those who are your enemies. The devil will not come with multiple heads or horns. He is much smarter. His potency is in his subtlety and secrecy. This is why the Bible says, *"But while everyone was sleeping, his enemy came and sowed weeds among the wheat, and went away"* (Matt. 13:25).

EXERCISES

A. If you were Adam or Eve, do you think you would have fallen for the serpent's deception? Why or why not?

Discussion

_____

_____

_____

B. Because God put enmity between satan and humankind (see Gen. 3:15), will there ever by a cease-fire in the war between the two? When?

Discussion

_____

_____

_____

C. Has the enemy ever used his subtlety and secrecy to sneak in and attack you? Your family? Your business or your ministry?

Discussion

_____

_____

_____

The God of Peace Crushes Satan

 POINTS TO NOTE

1. The Bible says the God of peace _"will soon crush Satan under your feet..."_ (Rom. 16:20). In repentance and rest is your salvation and in quietness and trust is your strength as espoused in Isaiah 30:15, and _"You [God] will keep in perfect peace him whose mind is steadfast on You"_ (Isa. 26:3). Do not be quick to resort to war. First, discern who is behind the mask—who or what is the source of the trouble. Do not accept fear or panic; rather, retreat into your spirit where the God of Peace resides.

2. Retreating into the spirit means practicing the functional components of the spirit in the midst of the storm and learning to remain steadfast in God, no matter the situation. You can do this by purposefully practicing the act of applying spiritual wisdom. This means applying the Word of God to real-life situations, using sanctified conscience by laying aside personal agendas and learning to prefer others, and supernaturally living in communion with God by spending quality time in His presence (see Phil. 4:6-7).

 EXERCISES

A. Do you allow repentance and rest to be your salvation and quietness and trust to be your strength? Or do you allow fear and panic to overcome your mind and emotions?

Discussion

_____

_____

_____

B. Retreating into your spirit means learning to remain steadfast in God, no matter the situation. Do you routinely apply spiritual wisdom to your everyday situations?

Discussion

_____

_____

_____

☙❧

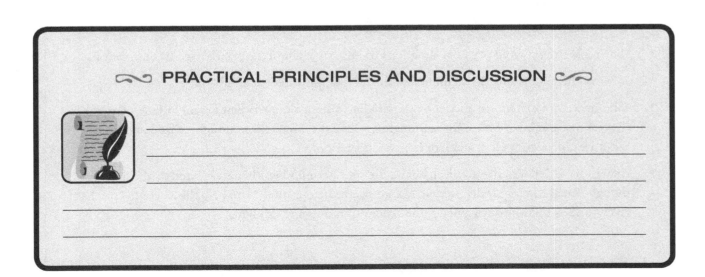

PRACTICAL PRINCIPLES AND DISCUSSION

CHAPTER 32

Fallen Humanity in a Fallen Earth

 POINTS TO NOTE

1. The fallen earth is a far cry from the original design of God for life on earth. Adam's fall affected the whole creation—a shadow of fear and dread that continues to spread even to this day. Not only was our relationship with God altered, but our relationship with the earth and with one another also shifted to disharmony. The present state of the fallen earth is described in Isaiah 45:18, Romans 8:20, and Second Peter 3:4-7.

2. In this fallen state, natural, zoological, and meteorological disharmony now exists. Death, disease, discord, sin, and disaster are all because of disobedience. The devil is enraged because God gave the dominion of the earth to man. We must fight him and also retain the order and beauty of the creation for the service of God.

3. The devil unleashed his evil strategy against Adam and Eve, and even today uses these ways to attempt to enter our lives (see Gen. 3:1-8):

   • Unguarded interaction with the devil (or evil).

   • Listening to the devil or pondering evil thoughts.

   • Copying the exaggeration of the devil (what you spend time on, you make room for; Eve exaggerated by saying "must not touch" the forbidden fruits).

   • Covet the forbidden fruits, persistent desire for evil things.

   • Saw the forbidden fruit was good for food (desire or lust of flesh).

   • "Pleasing to eyes" (lust of the eyes).

   • "Desirable for gaining wisdom" (wisdom of the world).

   • "She took some" (avoid places or situations where you will find it difficult to resist temptation).

   • "She ate them" (she finally succumbed to the temptation and disobeyed God).

   • "She gave them to her husband who was with her" (discussion between Eve and the serpent was in the realm of the "invisible" spirit; a thought-to-thought interaction; thoughts that come to your mind are either from God, satan, or human inspiration).

   • Adam was with her in the physical, but all the time her mind was being polluted by the devil even though Adam was physically present. We must prepare our minds and help those whom God has given to us so that the devil will not influence our minds and thoughts.

- "He ate it" (Once the forbidden got into the hands of Adam, it was irresistible. The eyes and imagination of men are major gateways for entry—good or bad. Hearing and thought processing are major gateways for entry into women.)

 EXERCISES

A. List several ways your relationship with God and nature was altered and shifted to disharmony because of Adam's fall.

Discussion

_____

_____

_____

B. The devil wants to destroy the present earth before the time appointed by God for the earth to pass away. Why?

Discussion

_____

_____

_____

C. Do you think Adam could have done more to help Eve resist the serpent's deception?

Discussion

_____

_____

_____

Consequences of the Fall

 POINTS TO NOTE

1. When Adam fell, creation fell into disharmony and many despicable evils entered the earth including:

   - Disharmony

   - Enmity

   - Fear and unbelief

   - Humanistic ideology

   - Toil

   - Pain

   - Curse

   - Death

   - Thorns and thistles (physical and mental)

   - Shame

   - Accusation

   - Nakedness (loss of divine glory)

   - False wisdom of this world

2. Any use of the elements of the earth outside the purposes of God is of the devil and demonic. Gradually the devil wants to drag us into unchristian relationship with the elements of nature and into demonic worship of these elements. For the purpose of God the sun stood still for Joshua to ride triumphantly in a divine moment. It was for divine justice that the ground opened in the time of Moses and swallowed Korah and his co-conspirators. Jesus Christ rebuked the wind and punished the fig tree. These instances represent the correct and proper dominion over nature in the affairs of humankind on earth.

3. Satan draws inspiration from and worships the elements of the earth. As Christians, we must only relate to these elements from the place of dominion given to Adam by God and redeemed by the blood of Jesus Christ. Many religions worship the elements of nature. But God placed humankind in dominion over nature, not in servitude to nature.

EXERCISES

A. Are there any despicable evils on the list that have not affected you personally?

Discussion

_____

_____

_____

B. List other instances that represent the correct and proper dominion over nature in the affairs of humankind on earth.

Discussion

_____

_____

_____

C. Do you know people who treat animals, plants, oceans, and rivers as if they were elements to be worshiped and adored—above the Creator?

Discussion

_____

_____

_____

❧

❧ PRACTICAL PRINCIPLES AND DISCUSSION ❧

_____

_____

_____

_____

_____

CHAPTER 33

Battle of the Mind

 POINTS TO NOTE

1. The greatest danger of this age is the fact that we are facing an elusive enemy and constantly fighting a war with rapidly shifting frontiers. Many people who used to look to the Church for answers to life's questions, comfort, and encouragement, have turned to things like astrology, necromancy, witchcraft, and divination in search of non-existent, conclusive answers.

2. We are essentially spirit beings having a human experience and a yearning for spiritual assurance stemming deep from within our spirits. If we continue to neglect this fact, we will continue to allow many to suffer from the overwhelming crisis of identity, faith, and the failure to grasp the true essence of who they are in God.

3. Born-again believers can no longer sit idle while the enemy targets our children before they are even capable of proper articulation of thoughts. We can no longer feign ignorance of the pollution of our minds in the name of entertainment. We cannot sit back and allow evil to be celebrated and honored in the name of fun and revelry. We must now rise to the call of our time and protect our minds, as well as the minds of those who will become the torchbearers of the next generation. *"We demolish arguments and every pretension that sets itself up against the knowledge of God, and we take captive every thought to make it obedient to Christ"* (2 Cor. 10:5).

 EXERCISES

A. Do you know people who believe in and ascribe to astrology, necromancy, witchcraft, and divination? At work? At home? In your church?

Discussion

_____

_____

_____

B. What can you do to help the many who suffer from the overwhelming crisis of identity, faith, and the failure to grasp the true essence of who they are in God?

Discussion

_____

_____

_____

C. Are you ready to *"demolish arguments and every pretension that sets itself up against the knowledge of God, and...take captive every thought to make it obedient to Christ"*?

Discussion

_____

_____

_____

❧❧❧

The Spirit of Compromise Masquerading as the Spirit of Tolerance

 POINTS TO NOTE

1. Lukewarmness is an insidious cankerworm eating at the core of giftings and anointings of God's saints. In the name of tolerance, many have wavered and compromised the strict tenets of Christianity. Other dangerous infiltrations include the spirit of procrastination, spirit of compromise, spirit of laziness, and the spirit of stupor (excessive sleepiness). We must resist the spirit of compromise by living by the Spirit and not fulfilling the desires of the flesh.

2. Most Christians are oscillating between the desires of their sinful nature and the desires of the Spirit of God. It is on this middle ground that many are sucked into the relativity of the world system such as the notion that there are many ways to Heaven!

3. There are three levels of spiritual existence: the natural person (the lowest level of spiritual existence), the middle level (babes in Christ), and the spiritual person (highest level, motivated by love for God). After the Fall, the soul and spirit were pitted against each other in warring conflict. When the soul is strong, the spirit is diminished, and vice versa.

4. To have the mind of God means that despite the pressures of the natural earthly existences, the uncertainties of life on earth, the fears, the jealousies, and other forms of carnal mindedness, we have chosen to attain the thought life of Christ. The thought life of Christ is interwoven with the attitude of Christ and anchored on His humility, obedience, and servant-heart born out of love (see 1 Cor. 2:16).

EXERCISES

A. Have you allowed lukewarmness, the spirit of procrastination, spirit of compromise, spirit of laziness, or the spirit of stupor (excessive sleepiness) to rule your life?

Discussion

_____

_____

_____

B. Are you constantly oscillating between the desires of your sinful nature and the desires of the Spirit of God? Are you living on the middle ground, getting sucked into the relativity of the world system?

Discussion

_____

_____

_____

C. When your spirit is strong, your spiritual senses are sharp and you are able to engage correctly in spiritual warfare. Is your soul or your spirit stronger?

Discussion

_____

_____

_____

D. Do you have the mind of Christ? Are your thoughts interwoven with the attitude of Christ and anchored on His humility, obedience, and servant-heart born out of love?

Discussion

_____

_____

_____

∽∾∾

∽ PRACTICAL PRINCIPLES AND DISCUSSION ∽

CHAPTER 34

Defeating the Devil at the Mind Game

 POINTS TO NOTE

1. Our minds are life's battlefields. Therefore, we must understand our thought processes to be able to appropriate them for the purposes of God. The way we think determines the outcome of our lives. We need to choose what we think and constantly reflect on what we think. Thoughts are the seeds that will one day yield their harvest.

2. One of the ways the mind is influenced is via the world system. As James says, *"but each one is tempted when, by his own evil desire, he is dragged away and enticed. Then, after desire has conceived, it gives birth to sin; and sin, when it is full-grown, gives birth to death"* (James 1:14-15).

3. Another way the mind is influenced is through intrusion from satan. The devil can access and input the mind, *"the god of this age has blinded the minds of unbelievers, so that they cannot see the light of the gospel of the glory of Christ, who is the image of God"* (2 Cor. 4:4; see also 2 Cor. 11:3).

4. God also desires to influence our mind. The Bible says, *"Do not conform any longer to the pattern of this world, but be transformed by the renewing of your mind. Then you will be able to test and approve what God's will is— His good, pleasing and perfect will"* (Rom. 12:2). God also admonishes us to be made new in the attitude of our mind (see Eph. 4:21-24).

 EXERCISES

A. Is your mind influenced most by the world? The evil one? God?

Discussion

_____

_____

_____

B. Do you take authority over your thoughts?

Discussion

_____

_____

_____

C. Do you extol as King David, *"Create in me a new, clean heart, O God, filled with clean thoughts and right desires"* (Ps. 51:10-11 TLB).

Discussion

_____

_____

_____

⤜⤛⤜

Developing and Sanctifying a Positive Mind

 POINTS TO NOTE

1. Developing a positive mind is attaining the mind of Christ. A positive mind is a mind centered on Christ, a state of continuous God-consciousness, nurtured, and sustained in the eternal Word of God. A positive mind is also a mind that is balanced, resolute but teachable, open, and discerning (see 1 Cor. 2:16b; Col. 3:2-3; Phil. 2:5).

2. It is necessary to constantly bring our minds into a sanctified state—a state of being set apart for the things of God and made fertile for holy imagination! You sanctify your mind by focusing on the Word of God, dwelling on the imagery of the Bible, and avoiding pollution by worldly imagery.

3. The inner self is the soul and the spirit of the individual. When the control of the outer self is broken, the soul comes freely under the rule of the spirit. If we are not able to rule our emotions, sanctify our minds, and yield to the will of God, the inescapable consequence is a steady gravitation to carnality, notwithstanding the depth of the anointing.

EXERCISES

A. Is your mind centered on Christ, a state of continuous God-consciousness, nurtured, and sustained in the eternal Word of God?

Discussion

_____

_____

_____

B. Is your mind consistently set apart for the things of God, being made fertile for holy imagination?

Discussion

_____

_____

_____

C. Are you the ruler of your emotions, the sanctifier of your mind, and the director who yields to the will of God?

Discussion

_____

_____

_____

❧❦❧

Releasing Your Spirit Self to Full Potential

 POINTS TO NOTE

1. There are several ways to remove the hindrances of the outer self to the proper expression of the spirit self. One is by fasting, which breaks the hold of the outer self and allows the inner self to manifest expressly (see Isa. 58:6). Also, by applying the Psalm 32 principles, you can release the spirit self. Consciously make efforts to release the inner self as your outer self thickens with interactions with the world.

2. Factors associated with *deceit in human spirit* include the following:

   • Transgression in practical sense means rebellion against God and His commands.

- Sin literally means violation of the rules of God or missing the mark.

- Iniquity means moral depravity.

- Deceit means falseness or misrepresentation or habit of cheating or deceiving.

3. Factors that constitute *hindrances to gaining understanding* of what God says include the following:

- Failure to confess our sins.

- Lack of consistent communion with God.

- Lack of prayers.

- Lack of songs of deliverance (praise & worship).

- Lack of wisdom and understanding (as the horse or as the mule, which has no understanding and has to be held in check).

- Lack of faith (being controlled by the "bit and bridle" of life).

4. Only the regenerated spirit of those who are born again can engage in spiritual warfare; therefore, we must learn to strengthen our spirits. You strengthen your spirit by crucifying the flesh, studying the Word of God, and dwelling in the presence of God. The spiritual senses are sharpened by constant use (see Heb. 5:14).

 EXERCISES

A. List the principles you find Psalm 32.

Discussion

_____

_____

_____

B. Meditate on the two bulleted lists and allow the Holy Spirit to bring to your mind and spirit any area(s) you need to work out together.

Discussion

_____

_____

_____

C. Are you daily strengthening your spirit by crucifying the flesh, studying the Word of God, and dwelling in the presence of God?

Discussion

_____

_____

_____

∽◦∾

∽ PRACTICAL PRINCIPLES AND DISCUSSION ∽

_____

_____

_____

_____

_____

_____

_____

_____

_____

_____

_____

_____

_____

_____

_____

_____

_____

CHAPTER 35

Two-Kingdom Conflict

 POINTS TO NOTE

1. Because of the Fall, the only way the Kingdom of God now exists on earth is within the believers of Christ—those who have opened the door of their hearts and let Him in. The expansion of the Kingdom of God on earth is the salvation of souls. God has a heavenly throne, and from His throne He rules over all the visible and invisible.

2. The kingdom of darkness is a counterfeit kingdom established when satan was expelled from Heaven and expanded when satan usurped control of the earth. Now satan rules the air and runs a system of multiplicity of thrones, kept in the hearts of the unbelievers in such a way that everyone is enthroned in his or her own heart. Therefore, self-conceitedness reigns in the kingdom of darkness. But this kingdom will come to an abrupt end, just as it started.

3. The two-kingdom conflict is a state of either yielding to the Kingdom of God or, by default, yielding to the kingdom of darkness. There is no middle zone. It is either one or the other.

 EXERCISES

A. The Kingdom of God exists on earth within believers of Christ—are you one of those who have opened the door of your heart and let Him in? Why or why not?

Discussion

_____

_____

_____

B. Are you guilty of allowing self-conceitedness to reign in your heart?

Discussion

_____

_____

_____

C. Have you chosen to yield to the Kingdom of God or by default have you yielded yourself to the kingdom of darkness?

Discussion

_____

_____

_____

❧❦❧

The Two Kingdoms

POINTS TO NOTE

1. The real and true Kingdom of God is also known as the kingdom of light (see 1 Pet. 2:9-10). Jesus said, *"the kingdom of God is within you"* (Luke 17:21; see also Matt. 6:10). The Kingdom of God is in every believer. God has *"been pleased to give you the kingdom"* (Luke 12:32).

2. In Revelation 11:15, we are told that a time will come when the kingdom of this world will eventually be transformed into the Kingdom of God. Between now and when the kingdom of the world becomes the Kingdom of our Lord, there will be gradual but steady expansion of believers in God's Kingdom—this is the whole essence of spiritual warfare.

3. The devil and his cohorts are a devious, wicked, but defeated force of evil who are in a hurry to commit havoc because they know their time is short (see Rev. 12:12). We need to be alert and have discerning spirits as satan's ability to pretend is far beyond human comprehension (see 2 Cor. 11:14). The Bible admonishes us, *"Be of sober spirit, be on the alert. Your adversary, the devil, prowls around like a roaring lion, seeking someone to devour"* (1 Peter 5:8 NASB).

EXERCISES

A. Why do you think God is pleased to give us His Kingdom?

Discussion

_____

_____

_____

B. Have you witnessed the steady expansion of God's Kingdom on earth? In what ways? In what regions?

Discussion

_____

_____

_____

C. Are you keeping a sober spirit and staying on alert? Are you afraid of your adversary, prowling around like a roaring lion, seeking to devour you?

Discussion

_____

_____

_____

PRACTICAL PRINCIPLES AND DISCUSSION

_____

_____

_____

_____

_____

_____

_____

_____

_____

CHAPTER 36

Kingdom of Darkness

 POINTS TO NOTE

1. Let us now consider the counterfeit hierarchy of the evil forces that satan operates, *"For we do not wrestle against flesh and blood, but against **principalities**, against **powers**, against the **rulers of darkness of this age**, against **spiritual hosts of wickedness** in heavenly places"* (Eph. 6:12 NKJV).

2. At the apex of the hierarchy is the chief prince, satan himself, whom the Bible describes aptly as *"**the god of this age** [who] has blinded the minds of unbelievers, so that they cannot see the light of the gospel of the glory of Christ, who is the image of God"* (2 Cor. 4:4). Satan and his minions lost their ability to materialize, however, so they can now operate in the natural realm only by possessing human bodies, animals, or inanimate objects. They are disembodied spirits who can use an enemy or a friendly person or object to get at God's people.

3. The names of satan include the resister (see John 8:44), the serpent or deceiver (see Gen. 3:14-15), the devil, meaning slanderer (see Rev. 12:10; Job 1:9-12), the god of this age (see 2 Cor. 4:4), the prince of the power of the air (see Eph. 2:2), and the father of lies (see John 8:42-44).

 EXERCISES

A. What does Ephesians 6:12 mean to you? Rewrite the verse in your own words.

Discussion

_____

_____

_____

B. Does the god of this age have any control over you?

Discussion

_____

_____

_____

C. Which name do you think most aptly fits satan? Why?

Discussion

_____

_____

_____

❧❧❧

Rulers of Darkness

POINTS TO NOTE

1. The rulers and forces of darkness in this world want to dominate the earth. In the present era, the powers and global influences of radical *Islam* and *Hollywood* fit into this category. *Poverty* is also a ruler of darkness of the perishing world—it is a powerful weapon in the hands of satan.

2. *Principalities* are satan's governmental spirits and are the impoverished attempts by satan to create a demonic force that will be equivalent to the force of archangels influence earthly rulers, governmental leaders, and the political machineries. They are displaced and dislodged in the spiritual realm by repentance and prayers of the saints (see 2 Chron. 7:14; Acts 19:17-19).

3. *Evil powers* target policies, influence behaviors, cultures, businesses, economies, and the spiritual climate over a given geographical zone. Evil power can blanket a region with a specific influence that allows the evil power to dominate (see 2 Cor. 4:4; see also Gal. 3:1-5). Emotional and social lifestyles such as gambling, prostitution, stealing, and drug abuse emanate from the influence of this level of satanic army.

EXERCISES

A. How has Hollywood influenced the world toward the kingdom of darkness?

Discussion

_____

_____

_____

B. How many governments can you name that seem to be ruled by the satan's principalities?

Discussion

_____

_____

_____

C. Other than gambling, prostitution, stealing, and drug abuse, can you name other evil powers at work?

Discussion

_____

_____

_____

❧❧❧

What You Must Know About Demons

 POINTS TO NOTE

1. Demons could be described as the evil foot soldiers of principalities and evil powers of satan's army. They seek to dwell in people or reluctantly in animals or in idols. Any believer filled with the Holy Ghost is able to cast out these demons.

2. Demons are real spiritual beings—not figments of imagination or mythological creatures. They are always contrary to God's objectives and oppose God's purpose and plans on earth. The Bible says they can cause affliction on people with physical symptoms such as deafness, blindness, or bodily deformities—but not all afflictions are demonic. Demons are associated with mental and emotional disturbances.

3. Understanding how demons work is important. Although some of the following twelve aspects were cited in Chapter 7, they are worth repeating. Pay close attention as knowledge is the best weapon against such beings.

    *   Demons have personalities and hence they have names. They can see, feel, and reason. In addition, they drive, push, or compel their victims.

    *   Demons are self-conscious and often very knowledgeable. The sons of Sceva had more than they bargained for when they met with knowledgeable demons (see Acts 19:13-16a).

    *   Demons need homes because they are disembodied spirits (see Matt. 12:43-45a).

    *   Demons have memory, can assess, work in unity, and have a sense of territorial domain.

    *   Demons operate a highly organized structure of orders and ranks (see Mark 9:28-29).

- Demons are capable of taking control of certain areas of one's life, but rarely do they take total control of a person. The story of the demoniac of Gerasenes illustrates a person who was totally taken over by demons (see Mark 5:1-13).

- Demons have desires and can make decisions: *"I will return to the house I left..."* (Matt. 12:44).

- Demons are cast out by the Word of God (see Matt. 8:14-16).

- Demons believe there is one God (see James 2:19).

- Demons are neither omnipresent, omniscient, nor omnipotent.

- Satan and demons can only act within the divine permission allowed by God (see Job 1:12a; Rev. 9:2-6).

- There are millions of fallen angels—so many that the earth and humanity would have long ago been destroyed if God had allowed all of them freedom to roam about and deceive and destroy humanity. But in His wisdom, God only permitted satan to have a small amount of fallen angels to do his bidding, enough to test humankind. Many are locked in abyss. I believe many more deadly demons will be unleashed later (see Rev. 9:7-11).

 EXERCISES

A. Have you known someone who was or is demon-possessed?

Discussion

_____

_____

_____

B. How comfortable are you reading, speaking, or even thinking about demons?

Discussion

_____

_____

_____

C. Why is understanding how demons work important for a Christian?

Discussion

_____

_____

_____

Spiritual Forces Hierarchy

 POINTS TO NOTE

1. The following table shows the divine order of spiritual forces, and compares it to the counterfeited hierarchy of satan's evil forces.

Divine Spiritual Force	Satanic Counterfeit Force
Colossians 1:16-17	**Ephesians 6:12**
For by Him all things were created: things in heaven and on earth, visible and invisible, whether thrones or powers or rulers or authorities; all things were created by Him and for Him. He is before all things, and in Him all things hold together.	*For our struggle is not against flesh and blood, but against the rulers, against the authorities, against the powers of this dark world and against the spiritual forces of evil in the heavenly realms.*
Kingdom of God **Daniel 2:44** *In the time of those kings, the God of heaven will set up a kingdom that will never be destroyed, nor will it be left to another people. It will crush all those kingdoms and bring them to an end, but it will itself endure forever.* **Revelation 11:15** *The seventh angel sounded his trumpet, and there were loud voices in heaven, which said: "The kingdom of the world has become the kingdom of our Lord and of His Christ, and He will reign for ever and ever.*	**Kingdom of This World** Lucifer was dealt with as an evil principality, but after his defeat, he was cursed by God and became known as satan. He acquired a nature of deception and distrust. In his fallen state, he set up a counterfeit kingdom and deceitfully became the prince of this world. Satan is not equal or opposite to God.

Children of Light of This World	Rulers of Darkness of This World
Christianity (children of light).	Islam, Hollywood, poverty.
Ephesians 5:8-14	Controls other principalities and evil powers.
*For you were once darkness, but now you are light in the Lord. Live **as children of light** (for the fruit of the light consists in all goodness, righteousness and truth) and find out what pleases the Lord. Have nothing to do with the fruitless deeds of darkness, but rather expose them. For it is shameful even to mention what the disobedient do in secret. Everything exposed by the light becomes visible, for it is light that makes everything visible. This is why it is said: "Wake up, O sleeper, rise from the dead, and Christ will shine on you."*	
Archangels	**Principalities**
Revelation 12:7-9	**Lucifer** (see following table for the correction and edition): Isaiah 14:12
And there was war in heaven. Michael and his angels fought against the dragon, and the dragon and his angels fought back. However, he was not strong enough, and they lost their place in heaven. The great dragon was hurled down—that ancient serpent called the devil, or Satan, who leads the whole world astray. He was hurled to the earth, and his angels with him.	*How you have fallen from heaven, O morning star, son of the dawn! You have been cast down to the earth, you who once laid low the nations"*
	Prince of Persia: Daniel 10:13
	But the prince of the Persian kingdom resisted me twenty-one days. Then Michael, one of the chief princes, came to help me, because I was detained there with the king of Persia."
	Prince of Greece: Daniel 10:20
	So he said, "Do you know why I have come to you? Soon I will return to fight against the prince of Persia, and when I go, the prince of Greece will come."
Powers	**Powers**
Global ministries administering the gift of the Holy Spirit.	Pornography, drug addiction, and violence.
	Seasonal blanketing of a region with power of a particular evil.

Spiritual Authority in High Places	Spiritual Wickedness in High Places
• Heavenly portals • Revival spots • Church leaders	• High places in the Bible. • Corruption of the priesthood, e.g., Eli. • Pharaoh • Hitler • Evil royal monarchs
Saints of God • Faith • Encouragement • Healing	**Demons** • Spirit of fear • Demonic spirits, bitterness, unforgiveness, anger • Discouragement • Physical affliction
Divine Spiritual Force	**Satanic Counterfeit Force**
Archangel/s **Angel Michael** Revelation 12:7-9, *"And there was war in heaven. Michael and his angels fought against the dragon, and the dragon and his angels fought back. However, he was not strong enough, and they lost their place in heaven. The great dragon was hurled down—that ancient serpent called the devil, or Satan, who leads the whole world astray. He was hurled to the earth, and his angels with him."*	Principalities **Lucifer:** Isaiah 14:12, *"How you have fallen from heaven, O morning star, son of the dawn! You have been cast down to the earth, you who once laid low the nations"* **Prince of Persia:** Daniel 10:13, *"But the prince of the Persian kingdom resisted me twenty-one days. Then Michael, one of the chief princes, came to help me, because I was detained there with the king of Persia."* **Prince of Greece:** Daniel 10:20, *"So he said, 'Do you know why I have come to you? Soon I will return to fight against the prince of Persia, and when I go, the prince of Greece will come."*

 **EXERCISES**

A. What have you learned from this chart?

Discussion

_____

_____

_____

❧❧❧

❧ PRACTICAL PRINCIPLES AND DISCUSSION ❧

_____

_____

_____

_____

_____

_____

_____

_____

_____

_____

_____

_____

_____

_____

_____

CHAPTER 37

Other Invisible Realms of Hell

 ## POINTS TO NOTE

1. In addition to the heavenly realms, there are also the invisible realms of hell. In the underworld there are these places mentioned in the Bible:

    *   *Sheol* (refers to the grave, death itself, or the place of burial. However, the term *sheol* connotes a common place, rather than an individual burial place. See Ps. 16:10; Isa. 38:10; Eccl. 9:10, Job 17:13-16).

    *   *Hades and Abraham's bosom* were the temporary abodes of the souls of the dead before the resurrection of Jesus Christ. Everyone will experience death, and the human body without the spirit will undergo a form of disposal. Before the death and resurrection of Christ, the soul of the wicked went to *Hades* and the soul of the righteous to the Abraham's bosom (see Luke 16:19-26; Rev. 1:18).

    *   *Abyss, the bottomless pit (Tartarus);* the abysmal region of Hades and also the temporary prison for demonic spirits. In this abode, these spirits lack the freedom to move around and therefore are unable to express their power on earth (see Luke 8:26-33). The word *Tartarus* was used only once in the Holy Scriptures (see 2 Pet. 2:4).

    *   *Hell, the Lake of Fire, and Second Death;* hell is the place of torment and eternal abode for satan and disobedient spirits—and, unfortunately, all unrighteous souls (see Rev. 20:14-15).

 ## EXERCISES

B. Which of these places come to mind when you hear someone spitefully say "Go to hell" to someone? Is it acceptable for a Christian to use this term when angry or upset?

Discussion

_____

_____

_____

PART V

How to Reach the Top

HOW YOU CAN LIVE AN EVERYDAY SUPERNATURAL LIFE

Introduction

Life is not a series of mountaintop experiences: even if it were, we are assured that the God of the mountain is the God of the valley; He who rules in the day is also the Lord of the night. Another thing I've learned is that whether circumstances of life attempt to strip everything away from anyone, there is one thing that cannot by taken away—our right of choice.

Ultimately the final outcome in our lives is the sum total of the choices and decisions that we make. My wish is that this section of the manual, as you wade through the intricacies of this life, will provide insightful inspirations to sustain and guide you in the right direction as you live an everyday supernatural life.

Unity, love, and sacrifice are prerequisites for living a good life. These important pivots of life also help us to translate personal experiences into good purposes and gains with corporate benefits. How this plays out in real life is like learning to tap into the deeper things of the physical life *and* of the spirit, because life in this physical existence alone is not enough for *"the letter kills but the spirit gives life"* (2 Cor. 3:6).

For one thing, if we want to make the difference and to inform people, we must know that genuine change comes only from the spirit. Hardship will eventually fade from our minds and memory; what will be more lasting is to emerge from tough times with a new and durable confidence in God's amazing love and to gain more insightful knowledge into God's wonderful nature and benevolence and to grasp the concept of the infinite goodness of His universal plan. We may never find answers to all the questions that life poses, but we know that God shapes the entire course of the history to His plan. Truly, as the Bible says, *"My times are in Your hands"* (Ps. 31:15). In all things, God works together for the good of those who love Him, who have been called according to His purpose (see Rom. 8:28).

Whether you are a successful entrepreneur, a pastor of a church, or a full-time housekeeper, you will find that if you, *"live by the Spirit...you will not gratify the desires of the sinful nature"* (Gal. 5:16). I have also correlated spiritual concepts with the mundane things of life on earth to highlight the relevance of spiritual principles in your everyday supernatural life.

CHAPTER 38

Living by Love

 POINTS TO NOTE

1. One of the hallmarks of a true disciple of Jesus is living by love so that all people can read the testimony of your life. Without love, you live in darkness; and when there is darkness within a person, it is almost impossible to navigate to your destiny (see 1 John 4:8).

2. Love and a reverent fear of God are connected. To fear God is to worship, respect, and love Him enough to desire to do what is right—no matter what. In reality, to love God is to never get weary of doing even the smallest thing for Him. God is not impressed with the dimension or magnitude of the work we do—He is with the love in which it is done (see Matt. 6:21).

3. We are not born with the spirit of love in our hearts. Jeremiah 17:9 (NKJV) says, *"the heart is deceitful above all things and desperately wicked; who can know it?"* By natural inclination, humankind's heart is wicked. Such a heart is set on the flesh, which is *"hostile to God. It does not submit itself to God's law, nor can it do so"* (Rom. 8:6-7).

 EXERCISES

A. How can you tell a true disciple of Jesus? How many true disciples do you know?

Discussion

_____

_____

_____

B. What does it mean to fear God? To love God?

Discussion

_____

_____

_____

C. How can you overcome the natural inclination of living, acting, and reacting from a wicked heart?

Discussion

_____

_____

_____

☙❧

The Dynamics of Love

POINTS TO NOTE

1. Romans 12:9-21 gives an excellent description of the dynamics of love in a very practical way. Love is the summation of all the commandments. The Bible also says that love is the epitome and the coming together of all the laws of God (see Rom. 13:8-14).

2. The practical aspect of love is putting the scriptural injunctions concerning love into practice in our lives. No one can impact or significantly influence another person without first showing compassion or doing it out of love. In the spirit realm, compassion and love always precede the miraculous.

3. Holiness comprises of freedom from sin being consecrated to God and living according to a divine spiritual system of purpose. Love on the other hand, transcends even the borders of goodness for it entails sacrifice and selflessness in a manner that goes deeper than goodness (see John 15:13). Indeed, there is no greater love! (See First John 4:21.)

EXERCISES

A. *"Love must be sincere. Hate what is evil; cling to what is good. Be devoted to one another in brotherly love. Honor one another above yourselves. Never be lacking in zeal, but keep your spiritual fervor, serving the Lord. Be joyful in hope, patient in affliction, faithful in prayer. Share with God's people who are in need."* Write these verses in your own words—then practice them daily.

Discussion

_____

_____

_____

B. Why is it that no one can impact or significantly influence another person without first showing compassion or doing it out of love?

Discussion

_____

_____

_____

C. What does it mean for love to transcend the borders of goodness and that it entails sacrifice and selflessness that goes deeper than goodness?

Discussion

_____

_____

_____

೧೪೦

The Reward of Living by Love

 POINTS TO NOTE

1. There is great reward in practicing how to live by love, and the Bible is replete with such instances. If we remain in love, we will rise above our circumstances (see Rom. 8:35,37).

2. There is power in living by love and an even more formidable power exudes from the love of Christ for us. God Himself works on the behalf of those who live by love and keep His covenant (see Rom. 8:28).

3. Jesus said: *Love the Lord your God with all your heart and will all your soul and with your entire mind and with all your strength. This is the first and greatest commandment. And the second is like it: Love your neighbor as yourself. All the Law and the Prophets hang on these two commandments* (Matt. 22:37-40). Here, God emphasized that the entire law and the prophets of God hang on the practice of living by love. The irony of life is that the greatest atrocities committed against humanity are traceable to those who have lost their capacity to love themselves, therefore rendering themselves unable to love others.

4. The degree to which you live by love is related to your responsiveness to the call of God in your life. You can correlate the levels of love with personal sacrifice and the calling of God in life.

Love with	Sacrifice	Calling of God
Heart (*Loving with the heart leads to the sacrifice of obedience*)	Of obedience 1 Peter 2:4 Romans 12:1	Salvation Romans 10:10 (*Sacrifice of obedience creates the way to salvation*)
Soul (*Loving with the soul leads to the sacrifice of praise and worship*)	Of praise Hebrews 13:15 Psalm 50:13-14	Sanctification Hebrews 13:12 (*Praise & worship enhance the way to sanctification*)
Strength (*Loving with strength leads to the sacrifice of service*)	Of service Hebrews 13:16 Philippians 4:18	Service Philippians 4:19 (*With sacrifice of service comes the call of God to His service*)

 EXERCISES

A. Is God Himself working on your behalf because you are living by love and keeping His covenant?

Discussion

_____

_____

_____

B. How sad is it that the greatest atrocities committed against humanity are traceable to those who have lost their capacity to love themselves, therefore rendering themselves unable to love others.

Discussion

_____

_____

_____

C. Meditate on this: Loving with the heart leads to the sacrifice of obedience, of which the first call of God is to salvation. Loving with the soul leads to the sacrifice of praise and worship, which comes with the call of God to sanctification. Loving with strength leads to the sacrifice of service; and with it, the call of God to His service.

Discussion

_____

_____

_____

Love and Forgiveness

 POINTS TO NOTE

1. No one can tap into the true measure of the fullness of God's power without the love of God (see Eph. 3:17-19). Forgiveness is the cornerstone of Christianity. The kingdom of Heaven was founded on the forgiveness that comes from the cross. The cross is the emblem of human unfairness, wickedness, and disobedience and also the all-surpassing love of God for humanity (see Luke 7:47 NKJV).

2. Jesus Christ made it clear that being unforgiving is an act of wickedness (see Matt. 18:23-35). In this parable, Jesus called the servant wicked and unforgiving; he was handed over to the jailers to be locked up. Forgiveness works on the release principle. First we have to release the person who committed the perceived wrongful act, and this forgiveness releases the power of love, which is capable of setting anyone free.

3. Forgiveness also works on a reciprocal principle (see Matt. 6:15). The measure with which you give is the same measure with which you will receive. The love of God is unconditional, but His forgiveness is conditional and proportional to how we forgive others. Forgiveness is an act of grace, not a reward for good behavior, so we should not forgive because of our own agenda. The acid test for spiritual maturity is how we love and forgive others.

 **EXERCISES**

A. *Forgiveness is the cornerstone of Christianity.* This is a truth—expand its meaning in your own words.

Discussion

_____

_____

_____

B. What is the "forgiveness release principle"?

Discussion

_____

_____

_____

C. What is the "forgiveness reciprocal principle"?

Discussion

_____

_____

_____

❧❧❧

PRACTICAL PRINCIPLES AND DISCUSSION

_____

_____

_____

_____

_____

_____

CHAPTER 39

Living in Unity

Together We Can Make a Difference

 POINTS TO NOTE

1. Solomon's prayer in Second Chronicles 6 marks a high point in the unity of Israel as a nation. With one mind, one spirit, and one heart, the nation came together in worship at the glittering new temple; and the supernatural coexistence, the unseen realm of God, became visible to mere mortals. The result was a display of the awesome power of God. They saw the fire of God come down from Heaven and the glory of the Lord in the form of a dark cloud filled the temple (see 2 Chron. 7:2-3). Acts 2:1-4 records a similar occurrence.

2. These glorious manifestations of His presence teach us many things; but most importantly, they teach us that it is time to lay aside those things that divide us and practice instead the things that lead to mutual edification and peace. For the Bible says how pleasant it is when brethren dwell together in unity and it's there that God commands His blessing (see Ps. 133:1). The blessing of God is the power to obtain the desired results.

3. Power comes when we are united in purpose, mind, and heart. In Acts 4:24 *"They raised voices together,"* and the Lord answered with an earthquake. The point is found in raising many voices together, for it shows the beauty and power of diversity coming together, and that there are certain spheres of the spiritual realm that we can only penetrate if we are in unity.

 EXERCISES

A. "With one mind, one spirit, and one heart, the nation came together in worship." Can you imagine a time when a nation in today's world would come together with one mind, spirit, and heart of worship?

Discussion

_____

_____

_____

B. Do you agree that this it the time to lay aside what divide us and practice instead the things that lead to mutual edification and peace?

Discussion

_____

_____

_____

C. Raising many peaceful voices together shows the beauty and power of diversity coming together and reaching certain spheres of the spiritual realm that we can only penetrate if we are in unity. What type of voices are being brought together in the world these days? Are they focused on unity or disunity? Why?

Discussion

_____

_____

_____

❧❧❧

Friction and Brotherly Love

 POINTS TO NOTE

1. Friction is usually a sign of alignment of different parts of the Body of Christ rather than the signs of rancor. Therefore, we must approach friction in the Body with a positive attitude and see it as the blending of various gifts. After all, as a family of believers, we should realize that kindred feuding is not new. From Cain and Abel of *"Am I my brother's keeper?"* (Gen. 4:9) through to Peter and John of *"Lord, what about this man?"* (John 21:21), even to this day it thrives.

2. Some of life's situations are divinely set up, and we must be careful to discern the true reason for each of our life experiences. Often they may have been orchestrated to bring us to the next move of God in our lives. We must confront the issues as they come, in uprightness, humility (see Heb. 13:1 NKJV)—no matter what happens. Remember what Jesus said, *"By this all men will know that you are My disciples, if you love each other"* (John 13:35).

3. A tree does not make a forest. No matter how big it may be. Even the eagle in all its abilities needs a push to bring out its best. There are several things we could accomplish in our lives but, in the midst of all that surrounds us, there is always a central purpose, and a cause for which to live. Jesus put this better than mere mortals could ever put it, *"For this cause I was born"* (John 18:37 NKJV).

EXERCISES

A. Do you, your church, your family approach friction in the Body of Christ with a positive attitude and see it as the blending of various gifts?

Discussion

_____

_____

_____

B. Because some of life's situations are divinely set up, are you careful to discern the true reason for each of your life experiences?

Discussion

_____

_____

_____

C. There are several things you could accomplish in your life but, in the midst of all that surrounds you, there is always a central purpose, and a cause for which to live—are you fulfilling that purpose?

Discussion

_____

_____

_____

∽∾∽

The Power of Unity

 POINTS TO NOTE

1. In the Book of Acts of the Apostles, there are many instances when the power of the unity was displayed to the view of all present. Acts 4:24 says, _"When they heard this, they raised their voices **together in prayer** to God."_ And God replied with an earthquake that shook the place where they were (see Acts 4:31).

2. Notice in Acts 2:1-4 that the sound came from Heaven. How easily we connect with Heaven when we are united. Even before the tongues of fire separated and came to rest on each person, the Holy Spirit first filled the room in which they stayed on that day, ordinary people were transformed and empowered with extraordinary abilities.

3. There are certain levels of spiritual advancement that can only be achieved by the power of unity and this will happen only if we come together. The Psalmist testifies to the benefits of the blessedness of living in unity: *How good and pleasant it is when brothers live together in unity! It is like precious oil poured on the head, running down on the beard, running down on Aaron's beard, down upon the collar of his robes. It is as if the dew of Hermon were falling on Mount Zion, for there the LORD bestows His blessing, even life for evermore* (Psalm 133:1-3).

 EXERCISES

A. Are you accustomed to regularly praying corporately or most often by yourself?

Discussion

_____

_____

_____

B. Why do you think it is easier to connect with Heaven as a group?

Discussion

_____

_____

_____

C. There are certain levels of spiritual advancement that can only be achieved by the power of unity—this happens only when you get together with other believers. Does knowing this change your idea about attending church or home groups?

Discussion

_____

_____

_____

∾ PRACTICAL PRINCIPLES AND DISCUSSION ∾

CHAPTER 40

Living a Supernatural Spiritual Life

 POINTS TO NOTE

1. A life surrendered to God is a life of simplicity of heart (spiritual simplicity). God is delighted to see us come to a place of absolute spiritual simplicity, innocence, and dependency on Him, but this may be hard to attain in these days when times are perilous. Nevertheless, living spiritually was epitomized by the life that Adam and Eve lived in the Garden of Eden.

2. Adam and Eve's stay in the Garden of Eden was the age of innocence and a state of near spiritual purity. God's original intention was for His children to enjoy a state of childlike spirituality and honesty. Many of those who are experiencing the joy of dependency on God today are those who have understood how we must come to God as little children—come to our heavenly Father with confidence and boldness in transparent innocence (see Matt. 19:14, 18:3-4).

3. Our goal must be to regain and retain this state of spiritual simplicity that existed in the Garden of Eden despite the evils of the day. It does not matter what is happening each day as each day has something to teach us, so we should continue in the confidence of who God is, even on our worst day. The power of God in us is entrenched in our realization of the fatherhood of God and in a life of total abandonment to His sovereignty.

 EXERCISES

A. A life surrendered to God is a life of simplicity of heart (spiritual simplicity). Define simplicity of heart in your own words.

Discussion

_____

_____

_____

B. God's original intention was for His children to enjoy a state of childlike spirituality and honesty. Describe this state and everything it entails.

Discussion

_____

_____

_____

C. It does not matter what is happening each day as each day has something to teach you, so you should continue in the confidence of who God is, even on your worst day. Does this seem like an impossible possibility?

Discussion

_____

_____

_____

∽∾∾∾

World Complexities Versus Spiritual Simplicity

 POINTS TO NOTE

1. There is a connection between possessing a childlike simplicity and tapping into the nature of God when dealing with the pressures and doubts that may come across the seasons of our lives. A state of spiritual simplicity must have prevailed in the Garden of Eden, prior to the Fall, which allowed the level of intimacy that Adam and Eve enjoyed with God. Unfortunately, when they ate the forbidden fruit, their natural eyes were opened; they became self-conscious and acquired the knowledge of good and bad through the work of the activated soul. The activated soul slid out of the rule of the spirit and became separated from God.

2. This activated soul has a natural tendency to acquire earthly wisdom and human knowledge. Even to this day humankind is driven by the activated soul to expand its knowledge in a world that's regulated by the value outside the perimeters of God-ordained statutes. Flesh and the resulting increase in knowledge have continued to plague humanity ever since. Daniel alluded to the maze that has followed the increase in human knowledge when he said, *"Many shall run to and fro, and knowledge shall increase,"* in the end times (see Dan. 12:4 NKJV).

3. Thanks to God from whom all blessings flow that He has not repaid us with punishment that our sins deserve. Instead, He has, in His infinite mercy, put in place the process of redeeming humankind to Himself. Salvation is a process of bringing the activated soul under the rule of the spirit once again. It is a continuous process, so we are saved and are being saved. The times the mind, emotion, and the human will predominate, are the times when we are operating from within the soul realm, making it hard to discern spiritual things. God loves spiritual simplicity (see Ps. 8:2 NKJV).

 EXERCISES

A. What is the connection between possessing childlike simplicity and tapping into the nature of God when dealing with life issues and problems?

Discussion

_____

_____

_____

B. Humankind is driven by the activated soul to expand its knowledge in a world that's regulated by the value outside the perimeters of God-ordained statutes. Why?

Discussion

_____

_____

_____

C. Salvation is a process of bringing the activated soul under the rule of the spirit once again—it is a continual process. Are you in agreement with this statement?

Discussion

_____

_____

_____

Pride Versus Spiritual Simplicity

 POINTS TO NOTE

1. The opposite of spiritual simplicity is the spirit of the world. I refer to this as the spirit of Uzziah because it is typified by the spirit that drove King Uzziah to pride. This spirit has a reliance on the works of worldliness and achievements. God helped Uzziah to develop earthly systems to sustain his agricultural, political, and military prowess, *"As long as he* [Uzziah] *sought the Lord, God have him success* (2 Chron. 26:5; see also 2 Chron. 26:9-11).

2. If we want to see the Lord high and exalted in our days, we must take our eyes off the world systems. In the coming months and years, God will shake the systems that are currently in place, which perpetuate the spirit of Uzziah. To return to the power of childlike simplicity, we must first deal with the spirit of Uzziah. Power abounds in unadulterated and simple innocence, and we ought to return to this state of spiritual naivety. Then we will regain what the devil took from us.

3. It must be said that the only true Source of power is God (see 1 Sam. 2:9). Consequently, true supernatural blessing comes from the only true Source of power; all good and perfect gifts come from God, in whom there is no variableness or shadow of doubt (see James 1:17). On our part, we must approach Him with spiritual simplicity.

 EXERCISES

A. Have you asked God to help you destroy the spirit of Uzziah, which relies and puts faith in the works of worldliness and achievements?

Discussion

_____

_____

_____

B. Have you dealt with the spirit of Uzziah? Power abounds in unadulterated and simple innocence. Are you prepared to return to this state of spiritual naivety?

Discussion

_____

_____

_____

C. True supernatural blessing comes from the only true Source of power; all good and perfect gifts come from God. Are you ready to live a supernaturally spiritual lifestyle?

Discussion

_____

_____

_____

⟳⟲

Spiritual Simplicity and Walking in Humility

POINTS TO NOTE

1. God resists the proud but gives grace to the humble. Humility and pride are opposite poles in God's measurement. Pride is a sin against God Himself, against His very being, and against His sovereignty. It is like a fist to His face. It is also defilement to the nature of God and draws us away from Him. God will not use a prideful vessel, because He resists the proud and He will not share His glory with any other.

2. Pride is a sin that originates from human strength. It is the most dangerous of all sins, because it is cunning and deceptive in its methods and speaks of reliance on human strength (see Zeph. 2:3; 3:11-12).

3. Jesus said, *"Blessed are the meek, for they will inherit the earth"* (Matt. 5:5). Our legacy to the future generations must be in our testimony that reflects nothing more than the evidence of our total reliance on God. Like Samuel, let us be bold to say, *"Thus far has the Lord helped us"* (1 Sam. 7:12). God also said in Isaiah 2:17, *"The arrogance of man will be brought low and the pride of men humbled; the Lord alone will be exalted in that day."* Simplicity and humility entail learning how to give honor to God and how not to draw undue attention to ourselves.

EXERCISES

A. Why is pride like a fist to God's face?

Discussion

_____

_____

_____

B. *"Seek the Lord, all you humble of the land, you who do what He commands. Seek righteousness, seek humility; perhaps you will be sheltered on the day of the Lord's anger."* Why is this Old Testament verse so very to believers today—to you today?

Discussion

_____

_____

_____

C. Have you ever considered yourself to have a spiritual simplicity and a humble spirit? Are you willing to adapt those characteristics to live a supernatural life?

Discussion

_____

_____

_____

~∾~

PRACTICAL PRINCIPLES AND DISCUSSION

_____

_____

_____

_____

_____

_____

_____

_____

_____

_____

Conclusion

You are destined for the top—the top of your class, your pay grade, your ministry, your family's respect—whatever top level God's will is for your life, you can achieve it!

I hope that after meditating on the readings, considering the points to note, and completing the exercises, you are now ready to live a supernatural lifestyle each and every day. You now know how to handle the issues of life that come your way—and stand in your way—so that you can keep moving toward spiritual maturity. Nothing can stop you now!

God bless you as you journey on—upward bound!

Ministry and Contact Information

The Father's House is a family church and a vibrant community of
Christians located in Aberdeen, Scotland, United Kingdom.
The Father's House builds bridges of hope across generations, racial divides,
and gender biases through the ministry of the Word.

You are invited to come and worship if you are in the area.

For location, please visit the church's Website:
www.the-fathers-house.org.uk

For inquiries:

info@the-fathers-house.org.uk
Call: 44 1224 701343

Books by Dr. Joe Ibojie

How to Live the Supernatural Life in the Here and Now—BEST SELLER

Are you ready to stop living an ordinary life? You were meant to live a supernatural life! God intends us to experience His power every day! In *How to Live the Supernatural Life in the Here and Now* you will learn how to bring the supernatural power of God into everyday living. Finding the proper balance for your life allows you to step into the supernatural and to move in power and authority over everything around you. Dr. Joe Ibojie, an experienced pastor and prolific writer, provides practical steps and instruction that will help you live a life of spiritual harmony.

Dreams and Visions Volume 1—BEST SELLER

Dreams and Visions presents sound scriptural principles and practical instructions to help you understand dreams and visions. The book provides readers with the necessary understanding to approach dreams and visions by the Holy Spirit through biblical illustrations, understanding of the meaning of dreams and prophetic symbolism, and by exploring the art of dream interpretation according to ancient methods of the Bible.

Dreams and Visions Volume 2—NEW

God speaks to you through dreams and visions. Do you want to know the meaning of your dreams? Do you want to know what He is telling and showing you? Now you can know! *Dreams and Visions Volume 2* is packed full of exciting and Bible-guided ways to discover the meaning of your God-inspired, dreamy nighttime adventures and your wide-awake supernatural experiences!

Illustrated Bible-Based Dictionary of Dream Symbols—BEST SELLER

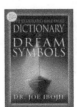

Illustrated Bible-Based Dictionary of Dream Symbols is much more than a book of dream symbols. This book is a treasure chest, loaded down with revelation and the hidden mysteries of God that have been waiting since before the foundation of the earth to be uncovered. Whether you use this book to assist in interpreting your dreams or as an additional resource for your study of the Word of God, you will find it a welcome companion.

EXPANDED AND ENRICHED WITH EXCITING NEW CONTENT

Bible-Based Dictionary of Prophetic Symbols for Every Christian—NEW

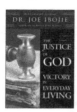

The most comprehensive, illustrated Bible-based dictionary of prophetic and dream symbols ever compiled is contained in this one authoritative book! *The Bible-Based Dictionary of Prophetic Symbols for Every Christian* is a masterpiece that intelligently and understandably bridges the gap between prophetic revelation and application—PLUS it includes the expanded version of the best selling *Illustrated Bible-Based Dictionary of Dream Symbols*.

The Justice of God: Victory in Everyday Living—NEW

Only once in awhile does a book bring rare insight and godly illumination to a globally crucial subject. This book is one of them! A seminal work from a true practitioner, best-selling author, and leader of a vibrant church, Dr. Joe Ibojie brings clarity and a hands-on perspective to the Justice of God. *The Justice of God* reveals: How to pull down your blessings; How to work with angels; The power and dangers of prophetic acts and drama.

The Watchman: The Ministry of the Seer in the Local Church—NEW

The ministry of the watchman in a local church is possibly one of the most common and yet one of the most misunderstood ministries in the Body of Christ. Over time, the majority of these gifted people have been driven into reclusive lives because of relational issues and confusion surrounding their very vital ministry in the local church.

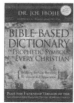

Korean translations:
Dreams and Visions Volume 1

Italian translation:
Dreams and Visions Volume 1

The Final Frontiers—Countdown to the Final Showdown

 *The Final Frontiers—Countdown to the Final Showdown* peers profoundly into the future. It expertly explores the emerging cosmic involvement of the seemingly docile elements of nature and their potential to completely alter the ways of warfare. Christians must not allow the things that are supposed to bless them to become instruments of judgment or punishment. *The Final Frontiers* provides you with a practical approach to the changing struggles that confront humanity now and in your future.

Times of Refreshing Volume 1

 *Times of Refreshing* allows you to tap in to daily supernatural experiences! Overflowing with inspiring messages, comforting prayers, and Scriptures that bring His presence to you, these daily boosts of God's love are just what the Doctor ordered for a healthy mind, body, and spirit. Best-selling author and Pastor Bishop Joe Ibojie and Pastor Cynthia Ibojie bring 365 days of hope and refreshment into your personal space.

Times of Refreshing Volume 2

 *Times of Refreshing Volume 2* gives readers the ability to tap in to daily supernatural experiences! As with *Times of Refreshing Volume 1,* Volume 2 overflows with inspiring messages, comforting prayers, and Scriptures that bring His presence home. These daily boosts of God's love are just what the Divine Doctor ordered for a healthy mind, body, and spirit. Each page includes a Scripture and God-given message, as well as space for interactive exchanges of the reader's written word with His. An added bonus is a listing of Scriptures to read the Bible in a year. Prophetic Prayer Points conclude this volume of encouraging and motivating messages of daily living the supernatural, victorious life in God's Kingdom.

Destined for the Top

 *Destined for the Top* presents simple and proven successful answers to life's most complex questions. Divided into two parts—Life Issues and Family Issues—you can be at the top of your game in every aspect of your life by knowing what and who to avoid during your journey to the top. Through an added feature of thought-provoking questions at the end of each chapter, you will learn how to strengthen your spirit, invest in your potential, and realize how fickle your feelings really are. You will discover how God's wisdom and love through you propels you toward fulfilling your destiny!

FREE E-BOOKS?
YES, PLEASE!

Get **FREE** and deeply discounted **Christian books** for your **e-reader** delivered to your inbox **every week!**

IT'S SIMPLE!

VISIT lovetoreadclub.com

SUBSCRIBE by entering your email address

RECEIVE free and discounted e-book offers and inspiring articles delivered to your inbox every week!

Unsubscribe at any time.

SUBSCRIBE NOW!

LOVE TO READ CLUB

visit **LOVETOREADCLUB.COM** ▶